Stunning. . . . A sober'-- look at the likelihood the USA survives the various at   made against her from withi

                                                        augh

In *America's Expiration Date,* Cal   bering message: that the United States is on the downward slope to self-destruction. You may agree with his analysis or not (I do not), but in view of the fall of other great empires throughout history, Thomas's injunction is well worth pondering.

—**Jay Winik,** author, *New York Times*
bestselling *April 1865* and *1944*

Cal Thomas brings a lifetime of working to save America and thinking deeply about what threatens us and what the lessons of history are. If we follow Cal's advice, America's expiration date will be put off for decades and decades.

—**Newt Gingrich,** former Speaker of the
House, US House of Representatives

I read Cal Thomas, always have, and have the utmost respect for the sincerity, depth, and insight of his work.

—**Peggy Noonan,** columnist, *Wall Street Journal*

In his timely new book, *America's Expiration Date,* my friend Cal Thomas shows clearly that unless we in America take seriously the grim lessons of previous empires, we are very soon doomed to follow in their footsteps. But by showing us just how those empires rose and fell, he makes our vital history lesson far easier and more fun that it might otherwise be. Bravo!

—**Eric Metaxas,** author, *New York Times*
bestselling *Bonhoeffer*; *Martin Luther*; and
If You Can Keep It; nationally syndicated
host, *The Eric Metaxas Radio Show*

AMERICA'S EXPIRATION DATE

The Fall of Empires and Superpowers . . .
and the Future of the United States

CAL THOMAS

ZONDERVAN
BOOKS
HarperCollins*Publishers*

ZONDERVAN BOOKS

America's Expiration Date
Copyright © 2020, 2024 by Cal Thomas

Published in Grand Rapids, Michigan, by Zondervan. Zondervan is a registered trademark of The Zondervan Corporation, L.L.C., a wholly owned subsidiary of HarperCollins Christian Publishing, Inc.

Requests for information should be addressed to customercare@harpercollins.com.

Zondervan titles may be purchased in bulk for educational, business, fundraising, or sales promotional use. For information, please email SpecialMarkets@Zondervan.com.

978-0-310-36348-4 (softcover)
978-0-310-35755-1 (audio)

Library of Congress Cataloging-in-Publication Data

Names: Thomas, Cal, author.
Title: America's expiration date : the fall of empires and superpowers . . . and the future of the United States / Cal Thomas.
Description: Grand Rapids : Zondervan, 2020. | Includes bibliographical references. | Summary: "Many Americans, regardless of political affiliation, are anxious about the future of the "land that we love." In America's Expiration Date, trusted political commentator Cal Thomas offers a diagnosis of what's wrong with the United States and prophetically reminds us that change will come when Americans look to God instead of Washington"-- Provided by publisher.
Identifiers: LCCN 2019034858 (print) | LCCN 2019034859 (ebook) | ISBN 9780310357537 (hardcover) | ISBN 9780310357544 (ebook)
Subjects: LCSH: Imperialism. | United States--Social conditions. | United States--Moral conditions.
Classification: LCC HN57 .T46 2020 (print) | LCC HN57 (ebook) | DDC 306.973--dc23
LC record available at https://lccn.loc.gov/2019034858
LC ebook record available at https://lccn.loc.gov/2019034859

All Scripture quotations, unless otherwise indicated, are taken from The Holy Bible, New International Version®, NIV®. Copyright © 1973, 1978, 1984, 2011 by Biblica, Inc.® Used by permission of Zondervan. All rights reserved worldwide. www.Zondervan.com. The "NIV" and "New International Version" are trademarks registered in the United States Patent and Trademark Office by Biblica, Inc.®

Scripture quotations marked ESV are taken from the ESV® Bible (The Holy Bible, English Standard Version®). Copyright © 2001 by Crossway, a publishing ministry of Good News Publishers. Used by permission. All rights reserved.

Any internet addresses (websites, blogs, etc.) and telephone numbers in this book are offered as a resource. They are not intended in any way to be or imply an endorsement by Zondervan, nor does Zondervan vouch for the content of these sites and numbers for the life of this book.

No part of this publication may be reproduced, stored in a retrieval system, or transmitted in any form or by any means—electronic, mechanical, photocopy, recording, or any other—except for brief quotations in printed reviews, without the prior permission of the publisher.

Cover design: Connie Gabbert
Cover photo: Pattadis Walarput / iStock
Interior design: Kait Lamphere

Printed in the United States of America

HB 01.22.2024

For Christie Jean ("CJ"),
who has put a new song in my heart

CONTENTS

PREFACE

Since the publication of this book at the beginning of the COVID-19 pandemic, events have confirmed what history, prophecy, and experience have taught.

Nations do not decline and evaporate all at once, otherwise people might wake up and do something to reverse the process. They die slowly and sometimes without people realizing it because they are preoccupied with trivial things—like celebrities and especially politics—and also nontrivial things, such as the promotion of behavior that God calls an "abomination." "If the foundations are destroyed," asks the psalmist, "what can the righteous do?" (Ps. 11:3 ESV).

The conflict today is not so much between truth and nontruth (because truth has been discarded in favor of moral relativism) as it is between competing antithetical moralities. But if moralities are competing and antithetical, how can anyone claim whether anything is moral?

Polls indicate that large numbers of young people are fine with behavior and ideas that would have disqualified one for a job fifty years ago, including the presidency of the United States. Many churches and denominations are embracing the attitudes of the world, apparently thinking that friendship with the world will attract more members. But they are losing members as people leave to join other congregations or simply reject faith. Virtually every mainstream Protestant denomination that has embraced the world has seen a significant decline in membership and donations. That should tell them something, but they seem more interested in seeking approval from the world than from God. These church "leaders" should be reminded of something late Roman Catholic bishop Fulton J. Sheen said more than half a century ago: "Moral principles do not depend on a majority vote. Wrong is wrong, even if everybody is wrong. Right is right, even if nobody is right."

This trend is not limited to religion. Consider what some major corporations and the Biden administration have done in the face of pressure from secular-progressive activists. These include the once-trusted Walt Disney Company, Anheuser-Busch, Nike, Kate Spade, BlackRock, police departments, and even the US Department of Defense, which have mandated diversity, equity, and inclusion (DEI) classes for employees and much more.

One bright light. The *Wall Street Journal* reported in July 2023 that some companies, including those I've mentioned, have announced that many of their high-profile executives who were hired at the height of the DEI trend have resigned or been let go. Some companies are also reducing their racial justice commitments. There are at least two reasons, I think. One is the growing weariness of companies that have felt they were drafted into the culture wars. They previously had as their primary objective selling products and services to as wide a customer base as possible. The other is the realization that emphasizing DEI cost them business because people began boycotting their products. The pushback from customers over Bud Light beer because the company hired transgender activist Dylan Mulvaney as their spokesperson, costing Budweiser millions of dollars as former customers abandoned it in droves, is only the most glaring example.

There is another decline that should concern everyone, regardless of political or religious commitments. A Gallup poll released during the summer of 2023 found that the share of people who say they are "extremely proud" to be an American has been falling for years. A majority of Republicans—60 percent—still claims extreme national pride, but the share has fallen from a height of 86 percent in 2001, when patriotism peaked following the 9/11 terrorist attacks. The last time Democrats said they were extremely proud to be an American was in 2013, months after President Barack Obama's second term had begun. It will be recalled that Michelle Obama said it was the first time in her life she was proud to be an American. This matters on several levels, not the least of which is voter turnout. If large numbers of Americans think it doesn't matter who wins elections or if they see the nation in decline anyway, why vote? This attitude becomes a self-fulfilling prophecy.

Another reason for declining national pride is what is being taught in too many public schools and universities. Too many have abandoned what our founders considered to be self-evident truths in favor of teaching that America is no better than any other nation and that the stain of slavery can never be expunged no matter what we do to rectify that injustice.

The great mystery is why so many Christian and conservative parents send their children and grandchildren to what I have called "indoctrination centers." We don't send American troops to Russia, China, or Iran to be trained. We train them here with our values and weapons. I have heard all the excuses, but none are credible. I have always liked what late First Lady Barbara Bush said: "Fathers and mothers [sic], if you have children, they must come first. . . . Your success as a family, our success as a society, depends not on what happens in the White House, but on what happens in your house."

Most important is what is happening in the spiritual realm. Polls consistently show that a growing number of young people respond with "none" when asked to identify their religious views. Despite history and scriptural warnings about the disaster visited on individuals and nations that forget God, Americans seem to be rushing at warp speed to repeat the mistakes of those nations that have previously collapsed or have been severely reduced in size, influence, and power.

What makes us think we are unique and can avoid the consequences of making the same mistakes others have made if we continue on our path? Ronald Reagan said we are only one generation away from losing it all. Each generation must renew the values passed down to it by previous generations or we risk becoming a byword in history. America has been an oasis in a secular desert, but that oasis seems to be drying up and the drought that will follow cannot be reversed absent a spiritual revival.

Politics alone, or even politics mainly, cannot fix what ails us. If it could, would it not have by now? That's because while we have a massive national debt, an open border letting in as many illegal immigrants as the combined population of thirty-five states, and the loss of a shared moral values system, our primary problems are not economic and political but moral and spiritual. It is why our leadership so often reflects what and who a large number of us follow.

If you doubt this, consider the devotion so many self-described evangelicals have for Donald Trump. Behavior that has been worse than what they denounced in Bill Clinton is overlooked when it comes to Trump. His devotees have settled for political pragmatism over moral principles.

"Righteousness exalts a nation, but sin is a reproach to any people" (Prov. 14:34 ESV). One of the definitions of *reproach* is this: "an expression of upbraiding, censure, or reproof." In the case of Trump, evangelicals seem to have abandoned the standard for righteousness. People have written me to point out that God used King David despite his adultery. Yes, I respond, but David repented of his sin, while Trump tries to justify his.

Recall what Paul wrote to Timothy: "All Scripture is breathed out by God and is profitable for teaching, for *reproof*, for correction, for training in righteousness" (2 Tim. 3:16–17 ESV, emphasis mine).

Are we listening? Are we learning nothing from history and thus doomed to repeat it?

No president, no Congress or Supreme Court can save us. Only God can, and only he might if we turn to him in humility and repentance. We must not combine him or replace him with the false god of politics and an overreliance on human leaders who make promises they so often don't or cannot honor. Again, will we listen? Will we learn? I don't know, but if we ignore or reject what history and Scripture teach, then America's expiration date will be more than a prediction. It will be a fact.

ACKNOWLEDGMENTS

Thanks to Jeremy Williams, my researcher, without whom I would not have the time to explore such history in depth. Thanks also to Lyn Cryderman, my editor, who helped me navigate all of the pitfalls that go with repeating myself and concentrating on the goal while writing my column, doing radio, and working on other things. Thanks also to the team at HarperCollins/Zondervan for seeing the potential for this book to warn of coming disaster (as Old Testament prophets did). One hopes we won't ignore these warning signs as the ancient Israelites did, suffering for their denial.

IF THE END WERE NEAR,
What Would You Do?

How would your life change if you knew the exact date of the end of the world, and that date was only a few years away? Just for fun, let's say you have received advance knowledge from a reliable source that on July 4, 2026, the world will end. Jesus will return on that date, the dead will be raised, and he will take those who have believed he is the Son of God into their eternal reward.

Stay with me. I'm not an end-times alarmist; I'm not peddling a particular millennialist view found through careful study of the book of Revelation. I'm a journalist, not a theologian. So please humor me and use your imagination. Pretend you're a character in a science fiction novel. That giant asteroid we've all seen in the movies is on its way. Efforts to nuke it off course have failed, and it's too late to try to ship us all off to colonies built on far-flung planets. The only help we've gotten from technology is the exact moment the world will go up in flames, vaporizing everything and everyone.

You may or may not have grown up in church, but you've heard the phrase "end of the world" through either sermons, sitcoms, or science fiction. *The War of the Worlds* was a famous radio drama in 1938. Some people listening to the broadcast narrated by Orson Welles on CBS believed it was fact. Many rushed out of their homes and into the streets, fearing Armageddon had arrived.

There was a time when church folk took seriously warnings about the end times. In the 1980s, a former NASA engineer, Edgar Whisenant, published *88 Reasons Why the Rapture Will Be in 1988*, mailing three hundred thousand copies free of charge to pastors all over America. An additional 4.5 million copies were sold in bookstores. When 1988 came and went without the archangel's trumpet blast, Whisenant published a new book, setting the date in 1989. Followed by another, setting the date in 1993. Then another, warning of a nuclear firebomb that would destroy the earth in 1994. By then, no one paid any attention to his warnings, which is why you may need to employ some creative suspension of disbelief to answer my questions.

How would you spend those next—and last—few years? What would you do? Who would you want to know better, love better? What would your bucket list look like? What offenses against others would you attempt to redress? Would you quit your job? And do what? Would you give in to greed, lust, envy, wrath, gluttony, and pride? One hopes not. Then again, what would be the point of love, joy, peace, forbearance, kindness, and the like?

If you knew life would end for you on July 4, 2026, what would you do?

Fortunately—or perhaps unfortunately—we don't get to know our expiration date, at least until it's almost too late to do much about it. You and I both know of friends or family members who have been given weeks, months, or possibly a year or two to live, but the rest of us not only don't know but also don't spend much time thinking about it. With little sense of urgency to motivate us, we live day to day, week to week. We get up, go to work, come home, enjoy our families, go to the movies, go to church, take vacations, and try to be decent and kind. Which is why plunging ourselves into my little scenario might be helpful, might shift our attention to what matters most in life.

This isn't a book about the end of the world. On that topic, I can't help you. But let's rephrase the question.

What if I told you I have a pretty good idea when our nation will breathe its last breath, or at least cease to be the bright and shining city on a hill that President John F. Kennedy mentioned in an address at the Massachusetts State House, borrowing from Jesus' Sermon on the Mount? How would you react if I told you I have received credible information suggesting that on July 4, 2026, this great experiment called America—at least the greatness part of it—will come to an end? What if I claimed that I have inside information indicating that on that date, America will join the once-great but now run-of-the-mill republics which stand for nothing, let alone liberty and justice for all? That the name America will be remembered fondly, but as a place to live and raise a family, the nation will be slightly south of ordinary?

I have, and my source is as reliable as he is courageous: Sir John Glubb.

You likely never have heard of him, unless you have a penchant for modern Arab history, and if you do, you understand why he is called Glubb Pasha. Or that he formed the Desert Patrol in Transjordan, consisting entirely of Bedouins. Or that in World War I, he suffered a shattered jaw, which led to yet another nickname, Abu Hunaik, Arabic for "the one with the little jaw." A career British soldier who led and trained from 1939 to 1956 what eventually became Jordan's army, Sir John also gained worldwide acclaim as a scholar and author, writing twenty-one books and hundreds of articles. One of them, *The Fate of Empires and Search for Survival*, is the inspiration for this book. Specifically, it was a paragraph from the introduction to that book that caught my attention.

The experiences of the human race have been recorded, in more or less detail, for some four thousand years. If we

attempt to study such a period of time in as many countries as possible, we seem to discover the same patterns
constantly repeated under widely differing conditions of
climate, culture and religion. Surely, we ask ourselves, if we
studied calmly and impartially the history of human institutions and development over these four thousand years,
should we not reach conclusions which would assist to
solve our problems today? For everything that is occurring
around us has happened again and again before.[1]

If that sounds familiar, you likely have read—and remembered—a verse from the Old Testament book of Ecclesiastes:
"What has been will be again, what has been done will be done
again; there is nothing new under the sun" (1:9).

Sir John's conclusion is the premise of my previous book,
What Works: Common Sense Solutions for a Stronger America.[2]
We have a history. We can learn from the past, not to return to
it but as a lesson for building a better future. Unfortunately, the
closest too many of us get to history these days is the instant
replay in a televised sports contest.

Sir John asserted we refuse to learn much from history
"because our studies are brief and prejudiced."[3] He was surprised to learn that the average age of a nation or empire's
greatness is 250 years. "This average," he writes, "has not varied
for 3,000 years."[4] Let that sink in. Over the past 3,000 years,
every great nation or empire lost its way in an average of a mere
250 years. I will do the math for you. On July 4, 2026, the
United States of America will be 250 years old. What makes
us think we will be protected from the fate of other great
nations, which often collapsed under the weight of financial
debt, moral rot, and military overextension? Doesn't it behoove
us—we who are living in the twenty-first century—to consider
how and why great nations have fallen, that we might guard

against the same fate for ourselves? Doesn't logic dictate such a step? And of far greater importance, armed with this knowledge, is there anything you and I can do to postpone America's expiration date?

If you knew that in fewer than ten years, this great nation will no longer be the beacon of freedom and opportunity it once was, what would *you* do right now to ensure that your children and grandchildren will continue to enjoy the uniqueness of America that was handed to you by your parents and grandparents?

Sir John found patterns, or stages, in the rise and fall of great nations. He called them the age of pioneers, the age of conquests, the age of commerce, the age of affluence, the age of intellect, and finally the age of decadence. Not every nation experiences each of these stages, and sometimes the stages have blended into each other. With some nations, it is difficult to distinguish between the ages of pioneers and conquests. But in general, each great nation or empire begins with some type of pioneer activity, gains territory through battle, and then settles into remarkable commercial activity, which in turn brings great wealth, and with it increased literacy and learning. All begin their final slide when a sense of shared morality and common virtue are abandoned. In the following chapters, I will take a closer look at some of the great nations of the past, to verify Sir John's observations regarding these stages and to show parallels. Then I will briefly look at each stage, to show some parallels with our nation and how they point to what appears to be the decline of the United States and the West, and where we might wind up if things are not quickly reversed.

You may notice that I will refer to some developments within these empires and nations that occur beyond the 250-year window indicated by Sir John. In most cases, the entity in question does not simply disappear after 250 years but staggers on in a much less dynamic and influential state. The important point to understand is that *they never return to their greatness*, and I believe that is our fate unless we take the necessary steps to reverse an almost inevitable decline.

As a journalist who has been commenting on our culture in a syndicated column for more than three decades, I can clearly see that we have entered the age of decadence, especially when one considers the characteristics Sir John attributes to this stage:

- Defensiveness
- Pessimism
- Materialism
- Frivolity
- An influx of foreigners [too many, too quickly to be assimilated, I would add]
- The Welfare State
- A weakening of religion[5]

Does any of this ring true for you? Would any of these characteristics describe what's happening in your community? Your state? Our nation? According to Glubb, decadence is caused by the following:

- Too long a period of wealth and power
- Selfishness
- Love of money
- The loss of a sense of duty[6]

Do you see any of these at work in America? "The life histories of great states are amazingly similar," writes Sir John, "and are due to internal factors."[7] It is my hope that by learning of these internal factors, we can begin to correct them in our lives as the first step toward reversing the decline of a great nation.

Georg Wilhelm Friedrich Hegel's famous line has become a cliche to some, but it is no less true. Hegel said, "We learn from history that we do not learn from history."

If America doesn't learn from history—our own and the world's—we are likely to suffer the fate of other great nations, rotting from within before either being conquered from without by an invading army or collapsing under the weight of self-indulgence, decadence, debt, a sense of entitlement, greed, and envy. It's up to those now living and the next and perhaps last American generation—and to those immediately following, should we endure that long—to turn things around. The late Soviet dictator Nikita Krushchev once vowed, "We will bury you."[8] Even he didn't foresee that while the Soviet Union would collapse, America might bury itself.

When I was a young man, a preacher—whose name escapes me—said that America is not at a crossroads, as some contend; America is a long way down the wrong road. We need to come back to the crossroads and take the right road. Historically, there have always been times when the US (and certainly ancient Israel) strayed from the right road and suffered the consequences for it. Most people are familiar with the story of the prodigal son, who leaves his father's house, spends his inheritance on wild living, winds up sitting among pigs and eating their food (the worst possible condition for a Jewish boy), and returns to his father with a repentant heart. His father has forgiven him even before the young man says he is not worthy to be called his son. This is a story for individuals and for nations, as we can read throughout human and biblical history.

The problem for us modern Americans, who have satellite navigation systems in our cars, is that we don't know where the right road is, because we have lost a sense of right and wrong and no longer submit to any authority higher than our own minds and life experiences. There is no right, and so we must tolerate everything, because to say no to anything gets you labeled intolerant or worse.

It is the height of hypocrisy for those who claim to be tolerant to be intolerant of any view but their own. These are the ones who strictly oppose censorship of any and all ideas, except those with which they disagree. It turns out free speech isn't so free after all. If your speech doesn't fit with the spirit of the age, you will pay a price. Sometimes it can cost you your job. In some countries, it can cost you your freedom. In a few, you pay the price for speaking out with your life. America is now in stage one of this familiar scenario. Canada is toying with stage two, prosecuting people who say things—including in sermons from pulpits—of which their government disapproves.[9]

What is to prevent America from sliding farther toward our own destruction? In these pages are some answers to that question. Let's not be like the people described in the song "Vincent," in which Don McLean sings, "They wouldn't listen, they're not listening still. Perhaps they never will."

There is no money-back guarantee on the United States. There is no certainty this country will continue to exist. Ronald Reagan used to say America is just one generation away from losing it all.

Are we that generation?

We could be, but I have hope that we just may be able to prove Mr. Glubb wrong for once. By the time we finish our study, you will also have hope.

CHAPTER 1

THE PERSIAN EMPIRE:
Today a Shell of Its Great Past

THERE CAN NEVER BE PEACE BETWEEN
NATIONS UNTIL IT IS FIRST KNOWN THAT TRUE
PEACE IS WITHIN THE SOULS OF MEN.
—*Persian proverb*

We begin our journey by exploring the rise and fall of the Persian Empire, which at the time was the largest the world had seen, but today all that's left is what we call Iran—hardly the empire it once was when formed in 550 BCE by King Astyages of Media.

Centered in what is modern-day Iran, Persia evolved from a series of imperial dynasties, not unlike many other empires. Cyrus the Great, who is mentioned by name or alluded to more than thirty times in the Bible, is regarded as the patron and deliverer of the Jewish people. He was the pagan monarch under whom the Babylonian captivity ended. According to Scripture, Cyrus was told by God to issue a decree to rebuild the Second Temple in Jerusalem and allow Jews who wished to return to their ancient land to do so. King Cyrus demonstrated his commitment to the project by sending back with the Jews the sacred vessels, which had been removed from the First Temple, along with a large sum of money to pay for building materials. He was today's Home Depot in reverse![1]

CAMEO: *Xerxes I*

If one needs an example from history of what harm military overextension and grandiose ideas can do to a nation, Xerxes I of Persia is a great one.

It could be argued, as many have, that most wars are unnecessary. Some wars are fought because the very survival of a nation is at risk. France and England declaring war against Nazi Germany after they were attacked is a good example of this. Other wars may be fought over a national interest that is not vital, like pride. The Persian invasions of Greece were launched not to protect a vital interest but ultimately because of pride. The conflict lasted on and off for nearly fifty years, between 499 and 449 BCE.

The Persian invasions of Greece were triggered in part by Athenian support for the rebellion launched by the cities of Ionia against Persia. While the rebellion was initially successful, a combined Persian army and naval force, once mobilized, was able to subjugate the cities once again. After the cities of Ionia were back under Persian control, Xerxes' father, Darius, attempted to invade Athens. Why? Greece had no great wealth or resources to claim at this time. The answer is because the Athenians had sent aid to help the uprising against Persia. Wounded pride seems to have been partially at fault. Darius was defeated at the famous Battle of Marathon, and while the Persian Empire could easily absorb such losses, its pride was undoubtedly wounded.

Xerxes was determined to avenge his father's defeat. He was like a bully on a playground. If someone weak stands up to the bully and manages to embarrass him, the bully must respond forcefully to maintain his position of dominance, even if it costs him more than the loss of pride he has already suffered. Xerxes launched a massive land and sea invasion of Greece and was defeated, losing most of his forces at the legendary battles of Thermopylae, Salamis, Plataea, and Mycale.

While the empire was as strong as ever, resistance by the Greeks managed to overcome what for them must have seemed like impossible odds. As noted by the *Encyclopaedia Britannica*, "The Greek triumph ensured the survival of Greek culture and political structures long after the demise of the Persian empire."[2]

The Persian Empire was able for a time to absorb the loss of a vast army and naval fleet, but there had been no existential threat to Persia, and so the calculation Xerxes I made was costly to his kingdom and his people.

The initial religion of Persia was Zoroastrianism—one of the world's oldest religions, predating Islam. In 651 CE, Arabs conquered Persia and established an even larger Islamic caliphate. Subsequent rulers established the Shia branch of Islam as the dominant religion. Shia Islam endures today under the theocratic government in Tehran. It was imposed in a 1979 coup led by the Ayatollah Khomeini. The nation is now called the Islamic Republic of Iran.

What I find fascinating about Persia is the number of concepts it practiced that are still reflected in modern cultures. Persia was basically a collection of nomads and thus did not have a central government, courts, a police force, or even laws. What kept them from falling into a type of anarchy was a code of honor that eventually morphed into a religion. The man behind this was named Zoroaster. He lived around 1000 BCE and introduced the concept of a singular god, the creator whom he identified as Ahura Mazda, bringer of asha—light, order, truth, the law or logic by which the world was structured. Not everyone in Persia at the time practiced Zoroastrianism, but such was its influence that the entire culture was shaped by it and embraced its ethics.[3]

Imagine a faith so influential that even those who do not practice it are shaped by it. That was once the case in America, where what some refer to as a Judeo-Christian ethic prevailed, but no longer. What would it take for our faith to regain that kind of influence?

A successor to Cyrus (by way of intrigue and murder) was Darius I. He too is mentioned in the Bible, in the books of Ezra, Nehemiah, Daniel, Haggai, and Zechariah. Darius was a man of influence and consequence in the ancient world and in the biblical narrative regarding the history of the Israelites. The empire established by Cyrus and Darius lasted roughly two hundred years but eventually succumbed to decadence and became a victim of the very multiculturalism it embraced, which included an army with troops who spoke different languages and were trained and equipped according to their unique traditions. This has obvious modern implications, because no nation can retain its character if it forgets what it stands for and allows too many people into the country while failing to assimilate them. A military coup in 401 BCE by Cyrus the Younger and some associates against his brother, Artaxerxes (who is also mentioned several times in the Bible, in the books of Ezra and Nehemiah), led to the eventual conquest of Persia by Alexander the Great in 334 BCE.

THE AGE OF PIONEERS

Not all empires followed the exact same path from their beginning to their eventual decline. Some have a clearly defined age of pioneers during which brave men and women forged new lives for themselves in new lands or developed new technology and stratagems that allowed them to take their civilizations to the next level. Persia is not quite like this. The Persian Empire was born in rebellion. The Persians already possessed a distinct identity and culture. What they desired was self-determination, freedom from the dominant power of the day. This, in a sense, was their pioneer period.

Ancient Persia occupied the same territory as modern-day Iran. Iranians still sometimes refer to themselves as Persians. In the early 500s BCE, Persia was ruled by the Medes. The Persians were vassals to the Median kings, and there is some evidence that Persians rebelled on more than one occasion. One of these rebellions was led by Cyrus II, a descendant of the perhaps mythical Achaemenes. Cyrus II (later known as Cyrus the Great) was successful in defeating the Medes in battle and drawing many previous Median vassals to his service. In a very short time, Cyrus the Great replaced a Median empire with a

Persian one. This empire is sometimes known as the Achaemenid Empire, named after its supposed progenitor.

THE AGE OF CONQUESTS

The Persian Empire entered its age of conquests as Cyrus the
Great immediately looked to expand his new empire. Initially,
he bypassed the Babylonian Empire and struck the empire of
Lydia, which was ruled by a man named Croesus. Croesus had
attacked the Persian city of Pteria after consulting with the
Delphic Oracle in Greece. Herodotus records in book 1 of his
Histories, a record of the Greco-Persian Wars, that the oracle
informed Croesus that if he went to war with Persia, a great
empire would be destroyed. As with the ancient Israelites, who
ignored biblical prophets foretelling coming disasters if God
was disobeyed, Croesus misunderstood one of several oracles
he consulted, hearing only what he wanted to hear. He also
ignored the advice of a top adviser not to go to war, resulting in
the empire's destruction. Cyrus had his generals conquer Asia
Minor after the conquest of Lydia, resulting in what is now
modern Turkey falling under his control.

Soon after the conquest of Lydia, Cyrus the Great attacked
Babylon, fulfilling Isaiah's prophecy regarding the fall of the
Babylonian Empire (Isaiah 13). Babylon quickly fell and
without resistance from the Babylonian armies, Cyrus ruled
all of what is modern-day Iran, Iraq, Syria, Turkey, Israel, and
Armenia.

Cyrus had put together his own version of a union, made up of
many tribes. He also engaged in a kind of religious pluralism and
tolerance that is absent today in modern Iran and in other parts
of the Arab and Muslim world. According to the *Ancient History
Encyclopedia*, "Cyrus, by contrast, saw cooperation as a strength,
particularly when it came to securing the main prize: Babylon.

The Military

The United States' military is the most powerful and sophisticated on earth. It is composed of some of the bravest and most selfless people in our country. Virtually all members join either because they love America to defend her against her enemies or to get help with training and an education for when they return to civilian life—or both.

Both motives are perfectly fine. Members of the US military are under the authority of civilians who are elected by themselves and their fellow citizens. Unfortunately, those leaders do not always use the military to its, or the nation's, best advantage.

Some examples: George W. Bush used the military to topple Iraq's Saddam Hussein and obliterate members of his Baath political party, creating a vacuum which Iran and the Taliban were eager to fill. That produced other problems, and not only in Iraq, which went through a period of instability as Islamic rivals battled each other for political power. At the end of 2018, the country seemed more stable, but neighboring Iran continues as the world's number one sponsor of terrorism, and the region, whose borders were created arbitrarily by a small group of men led by Winston Churchill following World War II, remains in turmoil.

Then there is Afghanistan, the site of America's longest war. While al-Qaeda, the terrorist organization behind the September 11, 2001, attack on America, seems decimated, its close ally, the Taliban, continues to surface from time to time, requiring additional military attention. Afghanistan is tribal and unfamiliar with the democratic processes of the West. Islam is a strong motivator, and many in the increasingly secular-progressive West don't seem to grasp the influence of the religion on its political worldview.

Another example is Rwanda. Bill Clinton said not sending the military to that African country to stop the genocide was a mistake he still regrets. Perhaps, but it's difficult to know whether US forces might have done more than temporarily suspend the violence without a permanent presence in the country, especially since white Westerners might have been viewed negatively by the warring tribal factions. An American force might have united the tribes against the invaders. And then there would have been the overwhelming cost and a further increase to the growing national debt.

When Margaret Thatcher was prime minister of Great Britain, she reportedly said that Westerners make a mistake when they transpose their morality on others who don't share it. This was George W. Bush's big mistake. Bush liked to say that freedom beats in every human heart. Unfortunately, many in the world have a different view of freedom than we do.

We can't use our military to impose a Western-style democracy on others. Each time this has been tried, it has failed. What about Germany and Japan, you might ask? These were nations that had totalitarianism imposed on their people and when free of those dictators and their ideology reverted to a more democratic system. Big difference.

We need to constantly review not just the purpose of our military but our role in the world. President Trump properly demanded that nations which have benefited from our defense umbrella since World War II start paying more of their share of the bill. Some have, and it gives them skin in the game.

We can't solve the problems of the world, so each challenge must be met individually. The blood and lives of our brave men and women (not to mention our tax dollars) should be committed only when the interests of the United States are at risk. There might be some exceptions, but that should be the rule.

Rather than trying to take the world's greatest city by force, Cyrus fought a propaganda campaign to exploit the unpopularity of its king, Nabonidus. Babylon's traditions would be safer with Cyrus, was the message."[4] The gates were opened, and palm fronds were laid before Cyrus as he entered the city, an activity that presaged another famous entry, on what we call Palm Sunday.

Cyrus implemented a policy of multiculturalism. While his conquests brought people from a variety of cultures and backgrounds, he allowed them to maintain their separate identities. As long as they paid tribute to him as their ruler, he would let them worship their own gods and enjoy their own customs. Cyrus II was a multiculturalist before multiculturalism was cool. More important, this policy helped forge Persia into a great empire.

THE AGE OF COMMERCE

As the Persian Empire continued its ascendancy, it entered a period of economic expansion, what Sir John Glubb calls the age of commerce. We hear a lot about infrastructure in America and experience it in numerous road closings and road work signs, delaying traffic and frustrating drivers. But that is not the only "infrastructure" in need of repair in America. There is also a moral and spiritual component that is crumbling. Darius the Great, who followed Cyrus, was big on physical infrastructure. It helped him improve trade throughout his empire. Among his best-known achievements were the Royal Road, a standardized language, and a postal service to facilitate written communication.

The Royal Road should be of particular interest to Americans. It allowed mounted couriers to travel from Susa to Sardis—a distance of 1,677 miles—in just seven days. On foot it took ninety days. The Greek historian Herodotus praised these rapid messengers: "There is nothing in the world that travels faster than these Persian couriers." He added a sentence that would come to be inscribed nearly two millennia later on the James A. Farley Building in New York City and is still today considered the official creed of the US Postal Service: "Neither snow nor rain nor heat nor gloom of night stays these couriers from the swift completion of their appointed rounds."[5]

Like other empires and nations that followed, Persia experienced prosperity as well as remarkable cultural achievements in art and science. Though what we know as Iran today is a shell of its former greatness, its influence from this period is still felt throughout Europe and other parts of Asia.

THE AGE OF AFFLUENCE

Commerce brings wealth, and it wasn't long before Persia amassed great wealth, primarily for its royal family. In addition to building the Royal Road, which enhanced trade with other regions, Darius initiated a standard currency, making it easier for him to collect taxes, which he used to finance great building projects and open new cities. Such was the wealth of Darius that he built an imperial capital, Parsa, with massive defenses protecting his riches. While small amounts of his vast riches trickled down to the masses, in essence Persia's wealth was shared by a select few at the top.

THE AGE OF INTELLECT

One of the benefits of the Persian Empire covering such a large area was the ability to gather leading engineers and other thinkers from all over the realm. This allowed the Persians of this time period to accomplish things that the early Persians could only have dreamed of. A prime example of their engineering skills was the approximately 2,600-yard bridge Xerxes built to move his army across the Hellespont in order to invade Greece. The bridge was a pontoon bridge made by linking hundreds of boats together as a base, then building a road across the top of the boats. Building pontoon bridges rapidly for military transport may seem difficult today, so imagine doing this without modern equipment and knowledge. Yet the Persians built this bridge and moved an army so large that it reportedly took a week for all the soldiers to cross it.

The Persians also benefited from the administrative skills of the peoples they conquered or absorbed. The book of Daniel records Daniel's service to Darius after Darius conquered Babylon. Darius recognized Daniel's ability and placed him in a high position within the empire (Dan. 2:48). Unlike others throughout history, the Persians seem to have prized ability wherever it was found, and not just within its original people. Regardless of the era in which they exist, bureaucracies require skilled administrators who devote themselves to the intellectual exercises necessary to run a vast organization.

Persia is no longer the first empire that most students of history look at when it comes to intellectualism. But ideas promoted in ancient Persia would eventually shape Europe and the United States, and that's why studying the subject is important. Knowing a country's intellectual roots helps shape and sustain any nation, or group of nations, even empires. Persia enjoyed statesmen, artists (Persian art remains impressive and valuable today), and intellectuals who promoted ideas that were precursors to modern thinking.

Rise of the Eggheads (Intellectuals)

The first generation of Persian intellectuals arrived later than those in Europe and Greece. They surfaced in the nineteenth century and believed Persia could not rely solely on ancient history if it were to survive in the modern world. These intellectuals encountered widespread opposition, as many often do when trying to break from the past. These men tried to establish relationships with those in power by creating blueprints they believed would lead to needed reforms. The rulers of Persia, like so many people in power, regarded these blueprints as a challenge to their authority and position, so they rejected them.

It would take a second generation of intellectuals to introduce modern civilization to Persia. This introduction came not just through a strategy of imitating the West but also through a coherent and systematic approach to European culture. By the time a third generation of Iranian intellectuals arrived, Soviet Marxism had infiltrated political and social thinking. In the fourth generation, Iranian intellectuals had moved away from imitating modern Western values and bowed their knees to encroaching Sharia law.

The overthrow of Mohammad Reza Shah in the 1979 Iranian revolution and the rise to power of the ayatollahs canceled what was left of intellectual pursuits in Iran in favor of the imposition of Shia Islam. Perhaps the mullahs were looking backward to the original Islamic conquest of Persia (637–651), which led to the demise of the Sasanian Empire (the name given to the last iteration of the Persian Empire before it was conquered). They certainly seemed to be going back in time as they imposed dress codes on women and beards on men and discarded any notion of free and fair elections. The mullahs, not the people, became the rulers and established what secular states would define as a dictator.

Following the Iranian Revolution, there was a cultural revolution similar to one that occurred in China that began in 1966 and lasted ten years. Like China's revolution, Iran's led to the imprisonment, torture, emigration, and massacre of Iranian scholars, not to mention the same treatment of pro-democracy advocates, who were jailed, tortured, and/or murdered when they protested the election of 2009, which many observers believe was fixed by the regime. The same treatment has been meted out to advocates for women's rights by a regime that believes women have only the rights the religious dictator gives them.

PERSIA'S AGE OF DECADENCE, ITS DECLINE, AND ITS FALL

Alexander the Great defeated King Darius III (who had become far less great) in 330 BCE, and Darius was eventually murdered by one of his own followers. While Alexander maintained the structure of the Persian Empire until his own death in 323 BCE, his defeat of Darius marked the end of what is known as the Achaemenid Dynasty, or the first Persian Empire.

When empires and great nations decline, there are multiple reasons that are usually interconnected. Such was the case with Persia. People who were not part of the upper class began organizing riots and other revolts against their rulers.

As this rebellion continued, Persian kings embraced "the dark side of the Force" and were perceived as working with evil spirits (Persian mythology viewed life as a struggle between good and evil). Kings became greedy (imagine that!) and started stealing from the nation's wealth rather than sharing that wealth with the people.[6]

The political structure joined the social structure in decline. Again, weak rulers created a political vacuum, leading to numerous provincial revolts, especially in Egypt, which hated Persian rule. Provisional satraps (regional officials) were becoming increasingly independent, some carrying on their own foreign policies (imagine each member of a US presidential administration doing that). They even waged war against one another. This constant infighting caused serious economic problems. Without a strong ruler who could train armies (and pay for them), and without an ability to gain wealth, the economy began to suffer.

Taxes were raised and quickly became oppressive, which encouraged more revolts and in turn led to more oppression, a vicious cycle. Persian kings started hoarding gold rather than recirculating it, leading to charges they were stealing from the people. There was also a decrease in crop production, which affected trade.

With limited resources, less attention was given to the arts and to buildings. Still today there remains a gap in Persian art because of this decline. It doesn't help that the mullahs who now run Iran show little interest in anything artistic or creative.

Finally, there was a decline in science, for which Persians (and other cultures throughout the region) had once been known. This decline in science and invention led to a reduction in weapons production, undermining the safety of the empire—the final reason historians believe it collapsed.

For a brief 250 years or so, the empire of Persia embodied greatness, which enhanced the lives of its citizens. During that period, I can imagine, friends were sharing meals and working alongside each other, thinking what they had would last forever: a strong economy, good jobs, robust contributions in art and science, a general feeling that all was well with the world. And then it was gone.

WHAT CAN WE LEARN FROM PERSIA?

What happens in Persia doesn't stay in Persia. If an empire as great as Persia can decline in such a short time into a shell of its former self, conscientious American citizens need to pay attention. No nation can survive on inertia, on the sacrifices and investments of past generations. Those qualities must be renewed by each generation, and sometimes within a generation.

Here's a little clue to consider. In Persia, the decline began after the empire experienced great prosperity. It seems that wealth can have a dark and negative side, though we shouldn't be surprised. Recall a Bible verse about the love of money being the root of all evil?[7] Of course, wealth is relative. On the personal level—which is where everything begins for nations—it's easy to look at someone who has more than you and condemn him as being consumed by his wealth. This is a constant refrain by some American politicians. The "wealth gap," they call it. The more pertinent questions cause us to look inward. Most of us are doing a little or a lot better than when we started. How have you changed as your paycheck has grown? The values of a nation are shaped by the values of individuals. Once Persia achieved prosperity and intellectual sophistication, it slid into a period of decadence. Is this inevitable, or can we collectively contribute to a kinder, more civilized culture by living out biblical values which have proved their worth whenever they are applied to nations and individuals?

What if people of faith live as they profess to believe? There are approximately 185 million self-described Christians in the United States. Granted, not all sing from the same hymnbook, but most would acknowledge certain biblical values, such as the Golden Rule.[8] Even a smaller number of believers in those values and principles can produce greater power. Large numbers of people, such as those involved in political movements, have displayed little power to redirect lives. Recall that the spread of the Christian faith began with one leader and twelve disciples and exploded to encompass much of the world. It did so not through politics or earthly power but with one person telling others about their need of salvation and the offer of a changed life. I recall a comment by the late Texas grocer Howard Butt. He was responding to the little red book of Chinese dictator Mao Zedong, which contained several of his quotations and Communist ideals.[9] Mao had said that power comes from the barrel of a gun. Butt said that real power comes from an empty tomb.[10]

Is that power and the use of it sufficient to postpone America's expiration date?

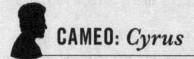

CAMEO: *Cyrus*

If Xerxes I was a bad guy for the Persians and so viewed in history, King Cyrus, who reigned over Persia for a relatively short period of time (539–530 BCE), was the opposite. The Israelites of that time could not have had a better advocate.

Mentioned more than thirty times in the Bible, Cyrus was a pagan king, demonstrating how God often uses people who don't know him, or follow his ways, to accomplish his will.

As I pointed out earlier, it was Cyrus who gave permission to the Jews to return to Israel after their seventy years of captivity in Babylon (Ezra 1). In one of the Bible's most amazing prophecies, Isaiah foresaw and predicted Cyrus's kindness to the Jews and put it in writing: "This is what the LORD says to his anointed, to Cyrus, whose right hand I take hold of to subdue nations before him. . . . 'I summon you by name and bestow on you a title of honor, though you do not acknowledge me'" (Isa. 45:1, 4).

This was 150 years before his reign! It also fulfilled another prophecy, announced in 2 Chronicles 36:22–23: "Now in the first year of Cyrus king of Persia, that the word of the LORD by the mouth of Jeremiah might be fulfilled, the LORD stirred up the spirit of Cyrus king of Persia, so that he made a proclamation throughout all his kingdom and also put it in writing: 'Thus says Cyrus king of Persia, "The LORD, the God of heaven, has given me all the kingdoms of the earth, and he has charged me to build him a house at Jerusalem, which is in Judah. Whoever is among you of all his people, may the LORD his God be with him. Let him go up"'" (ESV).

This is exciting stuff, but it gets better.

The prophet Daniel was among the Jews deported to Babylon (Dan. 1:1–7). He was later placed under the rule of King Cyrus, whom he served until at least the third year of Cyrus's reign. He likely, then, influenced the king's decree in support of the Israelites.

Besides his interactions with the Jews, Cyrus is also praised for his efforts in advancing human rights, his unsurpassed military strategy, and his bridging of Eastern and Western cultures. He demonstrated great influence and was miraculously used of God in fulfillment of Old Testament prophecies.

Not a bad resume.

CHAPTER 2

THE ROMAN EMPIRES:
Yes, It Really Burned

ON EARTH, GOD HAS PLACED NO MORE THAN
TWO POWERS, AND AS THERE IS IN HEAVEN BUT
ONE GOD, SO IS THERE HERE ONE POPE AND ONE
EMPEROR. DIVINE PROVIDENCE HAS SPECIALLY
APPOINTED THE ROMAN EMPIRE TO PREVENT THE
CONTINUANCE OF SCHISM IN THE CHURCH.

—*Frederick I, Holy Roman emperor*

THE FIVE MARKS OF THE ROMAN DECAYING
CULTURE: CONCERN WITH DISPLAYING AFFLUENCE
INSTEAD OF BUILDING WEALTH; OBSESSION
WITH SEX AND PERVERSIONS OF SEX; ART
BECOMES FREAKISH AND SENSATIONALISTIC
INSTEAD OF CREATIVE AND ORIGINAL; WIDENING
DISPARITY BETWEEN VERY RICH AND VERY POOR;
INCREASED DEMAND TO LIVE OFF THE STATE.

—*Edward Gibbon, author of* **The Decline
and Fall of the Roman Empire**

So much has been written by credentialed historians about the Roman Empires—one "holy" and the other not so holy—that there is little use in repeating their work here, except to say two things.

One, that these two empires do not fit Glubb's average of 250 years, and two, that they do fit the pattern of decadence leading to decline.

Historian Joshua J. Mark writes, "The Roman Empire began when Augustus Caesar[1] became the first emperor of Rome (31 BCE). The empire ended in the West when the last Roman emperor, Romulus Augustulus, was deposed by the Germanic king Odoacer (476 CE). In the East, it continued as the Byzantine Empire until the death of Constantine XI and the fall of Constantinople to the Ottoman Turks in 1453 CE. The influence of the Roman Empire on Western civilization was profound in its lasting contributions to virtually every aspect of Western culture."[2]

Rome's influence on the modern world has been substantial. That influence includes language development, architecture, religion (though also some pagan varieties, as well as the notion that the emperor was a god), law, philosophy, and even forms of government, such as the Roman Senate.

When I was in high school, the *Encyclopaedia Britannica* was the gold standard for research. It dominated school libraries and home bookcases throughout much of America. It still exists online and provides an excellent summary of the empire's history. I will not quote it at length here but instead call attention to the Imperium Christianum, or Christian Empire, which essentially turned the Christian church into an official state church. Imagine going to church on a Sunday morning where your pastor leads prayers and liturgies aimed at the president and the nation and suggesting that when the nation (empire) ends,

Christ will return and establish the kingdom of God. It was a fusion—or a political alchemy—involving two kingdoms, a merger that could never work and still doesn't function properly to the benefit of the church or the state. The temptation, then and now, is for the church to believe it needs an alliance with the state, either to benefit from favoritism (this is forbidden in the US Constitution) or to gain a sense of self-satisfaction, even superiority, as when fans of sports teams hold up foam fingers that say, "We're number one!" (Pride is forbidden in Scripture; it always goes before a fall, with both empires and individuals.)

THE AGE OF PIONEERS

"Big trees from little acorns grow" is a familiar saying that applies to plants as well as vast empires.

Little is known about the planting of the Roman seed. Most historians, after arguments about Rome's origins, now agree that the city was founded in 753 BCE and that the republic began in 509 BCE, following the overthrow of the last of its seven kings, Lucius Tarquinius Superbus. Don't you love the name, especially the Superbus part? These guys had a highly inflated view of themselves.

According to the *Encyclopaedia Britannica*, tradition teaches that the first six kings were benevolent rulers, but Lucius was a tyrant and was deposed by a popular uprising.[3] He would not be the last tyrant.

Most empires expand by forcibly seizing and occupying others' lands. Rome was no exception. As the end of the fifth century BCE neared, the expansion of Rome began. Population growth was a contributor, but so was war. The first wars were fought against a nearby town called Fidenae and against the important Etruscan city of Veii.

CAMEO: *Augustus Caesar*

The Roman Empire had seven emperors. Many people incorrectly believe Julius Caesar was the first. He was not. Julius Caesar never held the title of emperor. He was granted the title dictator by the Roman Senate because he held supreme military and political power.

Caesar's nephew and heir Augustus Caesar (or Caesar Augustus, as Luke calls him in his account of the birth of Jesus) was declared Rome's first emperor. The reason? He had destroyed Rome's enemies and brought stability to the growing empire. It was reason enough for the Senate to heap lavish praise on him and grant him a title that six of his successors would also bear.

Bragging like a modern politician, Augustus Caesar said of his accomplishments, "I found Rome a city of clay, but I left it a city of marble." In his forty-five-year reign, Augustus is credited with:

- significant legal reforms
- securing the empire's borders
- establishing Rome as a great political and cultural power
- initiating the *Pax Romana* (Roman Peace), a period of unprecedented peace and prosperity

Dreams of a greater empire were thwarted when a Gallic tribe descended through the Po River Valley and sacked Rome in 390 BCE. The tribesmen left after being paid a ransom in gold, but it took forty years of intense fighting in Latium and Etruria before Rome's power was restored and its expansion continued.

Following its victory in the Latin War (340–338 BCE), Rome assumed mastery of central Italy, spending the next ten years advancing its frontier by conquest and colonization. In less than fifty years and after three more wars, Rome dominated all of Italy. It was only the beginning. Remember, the Roman Republic was the entity that grew the city of Rome and prevented it from becoming just another city-state. The republic quickly evolved into an empire after the civil war that followed the assassination of Julius Caesar.

As I mentioned at the opening of this chapter, the trajectory of the Roman Empire does not fit Sir John Glubb's pattern as neatly as the trajectories of other empires do. In the next section, we will examine the ages of intellect and commerce together (skipping the age of affluence), with knowledge that affluence was increasing among Rome's upper class.

THE AGES OF INTELLECT AND COMMERCE

Visitors to archaeological sites in Israel (especially Masada in the Negev Desert) have seen the beautiful mosaic tiles Romans built for their baths and for their beauty. What would you expect from an eternal city? They built things to last, and many of their structures have lasted far longer than what passes for quality materials in today's throwaway culture. Experts say it is all in the concrete, which differs from that of our time and is far weaker than ours, but for some reason Roman structures endured for two thousand years. Some speculate it has something to do with volcanic ash, but whatever the reason, it is remarkable that such famous structures have endured for more than two millennia, with little preservation effort until the modern era. Renato Perucchio, a mechanical engineer at the University of Rochester in New York, believes, "These really large projects could only be done with the appropriate bureaucracy, with the proper organization that the Roman Empire would provide."[4]

The Romans built vast highways long before America's interstate system or Germany's Autobahn, not only shortening the time needed to transport humans on horseback and in chariots and wagons but also speeding up delivery of food, wine, and other necessities. The Romans created the Amazon.com of their day!

Despite the efficiency of some—but not all—roads, other means of transporting goods were used, sometimes at lesser cost and greater efficiency. It all depended on how fast one wanted things delivered. ("Do you want it overnight, second-day air, or the cheapest way?" today's post office clerk asks.)

We moderns can choose between land, sea, and air for delivery of packages and goods. The Romans used land, rivers, and the sea, but the means were considered as modern at the time as ours are now. All three methods of transportation grew significantly in the first and second centuries CE and helped spur Rome's economic growth as well as its social, political, and military reach. Romans used their transportation innovations to ship goods both interregionally and internationally, applying both state control and a free market to manage and encourage a robust export trade.

Though trade contributed mightily to Rome's wealth, much of which was used to subsidize its growing army and their campaigns, there was a snobbery about it among the elites. Commerce and manufacturing, notes the *Ancient History*

Encyclopedia, were regarded as less-than-noble pursuits if one happened to be well off: "However, those rich enough to invest often overcame their scruples and employed slaves, freedmen, and agents . . . to manage their business affairs and reap the often-vast rewards of commercial activity."[5]

Ah yes, overcoming scruples. See, there really is nothing new under the sun.

THE AGE OF DECADENCE AND DECLINE

"Rome wasn't built in a day," as the familiar saying goes. Neither was it destroyed in a day.

As mentioned earlier, one can put on a toga or a business suit and still behave the same under certain conditions. Rome was like that. For two millennia, a city called Baia was what we might refer to today as the Las Vegas of the Roman Empire.

Baia was a resort town not far from Naples. It featured spas and pools tiled with mosaics. One resident commissioned a nymphaeum, a private grotto surrounded by marble statues and dedicated to earthly pleasures. One doesn't need to have much of an imagination to know what that must have been like.

According to the BBC, Baia was chosen as a retreat for many of Rome's great minds, including the famous orator Cicero, the poet Virgil, and the naturalist Pliny.

Tales of intrigue flowed from Baia. There were rumors that Cleopatra escaped in her boat from Baia after Julius Caesar was murdered in 44 BCE. Also, rumor was that Julia Agrippina plotted to kill her husband, Claudius, while in Baia so her son, Nero, could become the next Roman emperor.[6]

In addition to the decadence that swept over the Roman Empire, two other factors contributed to its decline and fall: overexpansion—biting off more than it could digest—and overspending. See what I mean about nothing changing?

At the apex of its power and influence, Rome consumed territory that extended from the Atlantic Ocean in the West to the Euphrates River in today's Middle East. Acquiring such territory was hard enough. Keeping it was even more difficult. The logistics were impossible. While Rome had a good road system, communication over so vast a space was increasingly difficult. The defense of its frontiers became very challenging too. Local rebels and attackers from without saw opportunity to challenge the empire's power and eventually its existence.

The emperor Hadrian was forced in the second century to build his famous wall in Britain in order to keep Rome's enemies out. (Does anyone else see parallels with other walls— from China's Great Wall to the Berlin Wall to a wall in Israel to the wall President Trump wants built on America's southern border? Not all have the same purposes, but walls throughout history have been used for good and for evil.)

As increasing amounts of money were inevitably provided to the military in an effort to hold on to power and to keep the empire's machinery functioning, a greater price was paid for ignoring the empire's civil infrastructure, and it began to fall into disrepair. Citizens don't like roads that are not kept up— streets unplowed during snowstorms, potholes unfilled.

Rome is a perfect example when it comes to unchangeable human nature. As Israel's King Solomon wrote in Ecclesiastes, "Whoever loves money never has enough; whoever loves wealth is never satisfied with their income" (5:10).

It is the same with empires when it comes to conquests and land. And it is the same with elites, who are never satisfied with what they have but constantly want more to satisfy their egos and sense of self-worth.

In the city of Rome and surrounding areas, common people suffered from living in a nation whose ruling class cared more about what was over the next horizon than what was on the people's supper table. The gap between the standard of living of average people and that of the aristocracy grew wider. (Sound familiar?) As would occur centuries later in Africa, Britain, and America, slavery contributed much to the Roman economy, but the working classes received little. Unrest and revolution followed, put down by military force. It was during this period that Rome made the transition from a republic to an empire.

No single event caused Rome's collapse, but a series of bad decisions and a refusal to learn from history were all contributing factors. The decline took roughly three hundred years.

Historians have selected 410 CE as one significant date. That was when the Visigoth king named Alaric sacked the city. This was followed by the deposing of the last Roman emperor by the German chieftain Odoacer in 476 CE and the demise of Justinian I, who in 565 CE was the last Roman emperor to reconquer the western half of the empire that was supposed to be eternal.[7]

WHAT CAN WE LEARN FROM ROME?

According to Edward Gibbon, the Roman Empire succumbed to barbarian invasions in large part because of the gradual loss of civic virtue among its citizens. (Does anyone else see a parallel with our modern day?) Gibbon started an ongoing controversy about the role of Christianity, but he gave great weight to other causes of internal decline and to attacks from outside the empire.

It took Gibbon six volumes to explain the history of Rome's decline and fall, but one paragraph pretty much summarizes why it destroyed itself.

The story of its ruin is simple and obvious; and, instead of inquiring why the Roman empire was destroyed, we should rather be surprised that it had subsisted so long. The victorious legions, who, in distant wars, acquired the vices of strangers and mercenaries, first oppressed the freedom of the republic, and afterwards violated the majesty of the purple. The emperors, anxious for their personal safety and the public peace, were reduced to the base expedient of corrupting the discipline which rendered them alike formidable to their sovereign and to the enemy; the vigor of the military government was relaxed, and finally dissolved, by the partial institutions of Constantine; and the Roman world was overwhelmed by a deluge of Barbarians.[8]

Have we learned those lessons from history? It would not appear so. Might we repeat Rome's mistakes? What evidence is there that nations and empires that take paths similar to Rome's (and those of other empires mentioned in this book) have been able to save themselves from the ash heap of history?

Rome had it all for a time, but only for a time. While some beautiful art and impressive architecture remain, much of the Eternal City lies in ruins. The prison in which the apostle Paul and possibly Peter were held is a hole in the ground next to the destroyed Roman Forum. It could be argued that what came out of that prison is eternal, while the empire that was going to last forever did not live up to its billing.

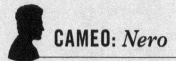

CAMEO: *Nero*

While no single person can be blamed for the fall of Rome, one person is perhaps best known to students of ancient history.

Most of us are familiar with the saying, "Nero fiddled while Rome burned." It suggests a lack of character and care for the people over whom this Roman emperor presided. His fourteen-year reign (54–68 CE) might be considered the showcase of Roman decadence, as well as a model of self-indulgent leadership. The fiddling quote is no exaggeration. He threw lavish parties even as Rome burned, plunging the empire into economic chaos from which it never recovered. It's no wonder, then, that upon learning of Nero's suicide, citizens ran through the streets celebrating rather than grieving.

Rome did burn, literally and metaphorically, and while Nero doesn't get all of the blame, he was part of a whole line of emperors who made significant contributions to its demise.

CHAPTER 3

THE BYZANTINE EMPIRE:
Officially Christian

If you're not clear on what the Byzantine Empire is, you're not alone. Even citizens of the empire would have looked at you skeptically if in the early 1000s you asked them how it felt to be Byzantines. As far as they were concerned, they were Romans. The Byzantine Empire is the term we give to the Eastern Roman Empire that continued past the fall of Rome and into the Middle Ages. The capital was not Rome but Constantinople. Citizens of the Byzantine Empire, which is also referred to as Byzantium, were not a new ethnic or political group. They thought of themselves as Romans, right until their annihilation at the hands of the Ottoman Turks in 1453.

So what's the difference between a Byzantine Roman and what we typically think of as a Roman? Some clarification might be helpful. The Byzantine Empire was the Eastern continuation of the Roman Empire after the fall of the Western empire in the fifth century BCE.

A Byzantine Roman bore allegiance to the emperor in Constantinople. Second, he professed the Orthodox Christian faith. Third, he spoke Greek. If you could subscribe to these three things, you were Roman, regardless of the empire with which you might identify yourself or in which era you lived. For them, to be Byzantine Roman was not to be born in a certain place or have a certain skin color. These three characteristics were the glue that held together a very diverse Byzantine Empire and its predecessor, the Roman Empire.

This glue raises an important question, and now might be a good place to begin thinking about it. America too is a diverse culture. What's the glue that holds us together? In your opinion and that of your friends, what is it that makes all of us, regardless of race or ethnicity, American? It is an important question, and the answer will determine whether the glue that has held us together through wars and economic downturns will continue to hold in the future. More on that later, but it is something to think about as we look at great empires and nations during the peak of their existence as well as when they are in decline.

The Byzantines were the successors of classical Rome. It's hard to select a beginning date for them, but I'll use 330 CE as the start because that's when Constantine I declared the city of Byzantium (later renamed Constantinople) to be "New Rome." Although Constantinople fell to the Ottomans in 1453, it suffered its mortal blow in 1204 when the Fourth Crusade, which was supposed to retake the Holy Land from the Saracens, was diverted to Constantinople and, despite a papal ban on attacking fellow Christians, the crusaders sacked the city. Latin crusaders conquered a large amount of Byzantine territory, which was eventually reclaimed by Byzantines, but Constantinople and the empire never fully recovered.

Many of the other empires mentioned in this book followed the same basic pattern as the Byzantines, who were the descendants of Rome and the Persian Empire, fought wars against the Arab Empire, and eventually were conquered by Ottomans.

THE AGE OF PIONEERS

When you play the classic computer strategy game *Age of Empires II*, there are certain types of matches in which you can choose your starting age, such as stone, feudal, or imperial. Players can even choose to perform a "fast start" that allows them to begin the game with large amounts of resources and money. That is what the Byzantines were blessed with. They inherited from Rome an established, wealthy, and successful state. The eastern part of the Roman Empire was the center of economic activity. Even at the height of classical Rome, the bulk of the wealth that paid for their massive public works and the legions that marched from Britain to Jerusalem came from the east.

Therefore the Byzantines did not have pioneers of their own. So the question is, why did the Byzantines survive and Rome fall? A comprehensive answer would require an entire book, but here's a short but not necessarily inaccurate answer: an emperor who knew what he believed.

In the third century, the Roman Empire was engulfed in anarchy. Rebellion stemming from issues of succession, famine, disease, economic instability, and social unrest hindered any one man, even though declared to be emperor, from ruling effectively. Eventually, a man by the name of Diocletian became emperor and, aided by another man named Constantine, stabilized much of the empire. Constantine was subsequently declared emperor, and his later life laid the foundation for the rest of the Byzantines' history.

Among the best-known decisions Constantine made to help stabilize the empire was his actions in regard to those who practiced the Christian faith. Most people are aware that Constantine legalized Christianity; what most are unaware of are his actions that helped the church to establish orthodoxy—specifically, the calling of the Council of Nicaea in 325. This council, or gathering of religious leaders, rejected a heresy threatening the church and affirmed the deity of Christ. It was at Nicaea that the council declared,

We believe in one God, the FATHER Almighty, Maker of all things visible and invisible. And in one Lord JESUS CHRIST, the Son of God, begotten of the Father [the only-begotten; that is, of the essence of the Father, God of God], Light of Light, very God of very God, begotten, not made, being of one substance with the Father; by whom all things were made [both in heaven and on earth]; who for us men, and for our salvation, came down and was incarnate and was made man; he suffered, and the third day he rose again, ascended into heaven; from thence he shall come to judge the quick and the dead. And in the HOLY GHOST. But those who say: "There was a time when he was not"; and "He was not before he was made"; and "He was made out of nothing," or "He is of another substance" or "essence," or "The Son of God is created," or "changeable," or "alterable"—they are condemned by the holy catholic and apostolic Church.

This became known as the Nicene Creed, and it is repeated in one form or another in many contemporary Christian churches throughout the world. A creed is simply a statement of belief, and by systematically declaring the essentials of Christian belief, this council provided the church a standard with which it could ward off current and future heresies. It served as a unifying force throughout Christianity and the empire.[1]

THE AGE OF CONQUESTS

The Byzantine Empire was always at war. Constantly surrounded by enemies, the empire regularly lost and then regained territory. Under the reign of Justinian the Great, the empire regained territory in Africa, Spain, and Italy. At the end of his reign, the territory of the Byzantine Empire looked much like that of the glory days of Rome. However, Europe had changed, and Justinian's wars pushed the resources of the empire to the brink. Europe's rapidly shrinking connection to its Roman past, paired with the invasions of the Goths and Vandals, meant that the territory regained under Justinian was impossible to hold. From then on, warfare for the Byzantines was primarily defensive in nature.

Between 602 and 628, the Byzantines fought a devastating war with the Sasanian Empire of Persia. Initially, massive Sasanian victories forced the Byzantines back to within the walls of Constantinople itself, and the Sasanians very nearly achieved complete victory in the 626 siege of Constantinople. However, the emperor Heraclius led a campaign into the heart of the Sasanian Empire, forcing them to sue for peace. At the end of the conflict, the two sides were utterly exhausted and forced back to basically their starting positions. This exhaustion made both sides vulnerable to the sudden emergence of the Arab Empire on the Arab Peninsula. Arab armies conquered the entire Sasanian Empire in short order, then proceeded to conquer Byzantine territory in the Holy Land, Egypt, North Africa, and the Caucasus. The Arabs advanced all the way across North Africa and into Spain, where they were finally stopped by Charles Martel and the Franks in 732 (which I will discuss later, when we look at the Arab Empire).

This dramatic series of setbacks caused the Byzantines to adopt a military strategy that allowed them to continue to survive and even to reclaim some of their lost territory. This strategy was called the theme system. Under this system, the empire maintained a small, elite professional army in Constantinople, while the rest of the empire was divided into administrative areas known as themes, each of which was led by a general. The theme was divided into *stratiotika ktemata* (soldier lands), where the government granted land to soldiers. In exchange, the soldiers agreed to arm themselves, provide horses, or serve in the army. As a result, soldiers had a real and direct connection to the land they were defending. It does not take a military strategist on par with Napoleon to understand that a man defending his own home and land is a far more reliable soldier than someone fighting for pay hundreds of miles away from his homeland. It is not inaccurate to compare them to the minutemen of the British colonies, men who maintained their own arms and had to be ready to fight at a moment's notice.

If a theme was invaded, the local general pulled together as many local soldiers as he needed to resist the invasion. When faced with larger invasions, multiple themes would come together, aided by the professional army from Constantinople. This flexible system was modified throughout the empire's history but served as the backbone of the empire's military strength for six hundred years.

THE AGE OF INTELLECT

The word Byzantine today is often used as a pejorative, conjuring up an era of ignorance and religious intolerance, among other conditions and practices. That's unfortunate and perhaps reflects an antireligious bias. Admittedly, Byzantine art was created primarily to inspire religious devotion, but over the centuries it has stood the test of time. Its icons are still considered to be among the most beautiful ever created, and Byzantine architecture continues to inspire awe and admiration, even from unbelievers. Throughout history, much of the great art was commissioned by the church through faithful benefactors who saw beauty as a reflection of their faith. By contrast, the emphasis today in much of the art world seems to be on trying to shock and desensitize with the most disturbing of subject matter. As they say, beauty is in the eye of the beholder, and to the Byzantines, art reflected the beauty of their faith.

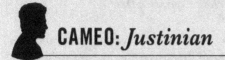

CAMEO: *Justinian*

By far, the most influential and consequential leader of the time was Justinian the Great (who thereby richly deserved his honorific). The list of his accomplishments is long. More than anyone else, Justinian was responsible for expanding the empire. Let me qualify that. Justinian had a wealthy and strong wife.[2] Her name was Theodora. She was "probably the most powerful woman in Byzantine history."

The Byzantines were burdened by high taxes, which made them unhappy. (Sound familiar?) Their unhappiness led to riots in the streets. Using a version of Roman law, Justinian curtailed the riots, restoring law and order, and began the rebuilding of Constantinople. The most visible and enduring contribution of Justinian was the Hagia Sophia. This monument to the Christian faith has been described as "one of the most extraordinary marvels in the eastern world."[3]

If the success of a leader can be judged by how much land they grab, Justinian gets a gold medal. He conquered not only Italy but also much of the North African coast. His reach extended as far as Spain.

While Abraham Lincoln used a "team of rivals," as historian Doris Kearns Goodwin called them, Justinian used his wife and close associates to advance his vision. In addition to seeking the aid and advice of Theodora, who was the prototype of a strong woman, he was secure enough in his power and position to grant his general, Belisarius, authority to handle military operations. Justinian was "brilliant and cunning" and "took full advantage of those around him."[4]

Byzantium also can be credited with caring about and caring for important works of literature. The Byzantine Empire has been credited for not only preserving great literary works of the past but also creating their own literature. As contemporary librarian and archivist Barbara J. Ilie observed, "The Byzantine Empire supported literary life at a time when many other parts of the western world were in a state of literary darkness."[5]

Like the Medicis and other patrons of the arts in Italy during the Renaissance, the leaders of the Byzantine Empire supported literary life at a time when many places had turned off the intellectual lights.

A prime example of the intellectual and creative forces in the Byzantine Empire is the construction of the Hagia Sophia (537 CE), a massive church in Istanbul ordered built by the emperor Justinian the Great on what he said were instructions from God. The name Hagia Sophia means "holy wisdom." The edifice began as a Greek Orthodox church and later was converted into an imperial mosque during the Ottoman Dynasty, enduring as a mosque for five hundred years (which we'll cover in chapter 6). In 1935, it was converted again, this time to a secular museum. You can't miss it if you are fortunate enough to make the trip from the airport into central Istanbul.

The church/mosque/museum is widely considered to be the touchstone of Byzantine architecture and remained the world's largest cathedral for nearly a thousand years, until the Seville Cathedral was completed in 1520. There is a story behind the Hagia Sophia's construction which is most likely apocryphal but is nevertheless fun to consider, if only because we can recognize our own human nature in the people of that time.

The narrative of how the Hagia Sophia was built comes from a tenth-century collection of stories and legends called the Patria. It is an anonymous account, which makes it suspect in the eyes of some historians, though in our day anonymous sources are treated in major media as credible. The Patria reads like what we would today call a travel guide for the Byzantium capital, offering dubious tidbits about how the church was built, including the Emperor Justinian's claim that God inspired him to build it bigger than any church since Adam's time. Hmm. Either God left that church out of Adam's story in Genesis, or the emperor was guilty of fake news.

Justinian faced the same kinds of glitches in his construction project that builders of today's modern arenas face—specifically, stubborn holdouts refusing to sell their property. In one case, the holdout was a widow named Anna, whom Justinian visited, only to learn she would sell her land on the condition she could be buried in the church. "Granted," said the emperor. A man named Antiochus was thrown in jail for refusing to sell. A lover of horse races, he shouted from his jail cell just before the great races were to begin at the Hippodrome, "Let me see the Hippodrome games, I will do the will of the emperor." He got to see the races, and the emperor grabbed another tract of land for his massive church. The stories gradually grew into legends, even with reports of angels showing up to guard the tools of the thousands of construction workers. Then again, I've heard a few doozies from preachers and politicians regarding kingdoms they've built, so I guess we can forgive Emperor Justinian for possibly stretching the truth.[6]

Sadly, the building of this great church did not protect the empire from forces that eventually render the mighty powerless to save either their empires or themselves.

DECADENCE AND DECLINE

The Byzantine Empire had to contend with the ancient enemy of Sassanid Persia and the new threat of Islam that came like a firestorm out of Arabia.

In 629 CE, the prophet Muhammad sent letters to the kings of Persia, Yemen, and Ethiopia and to Emperor Heraclius, inviting them to accept Islam. Muhammad stated, "If you become a Muslim you will be safe, and God will double your reward, but if you reject this invitation of Islam you will bear the sin of having misguided your subjects." It was an ultimatum, from an unknown "holy man" beyond the fringe of civilization to the most powerful rulers in the world.

People in the West who are not history buffs are probably unfamiliar with the name Heraclius. One reason is that we don't study history like we once did, though it is a guide from which we can learn lessons in our time. In the seventh century, Heraclius was the most powerful and successful ruler in the world. The Byzantine Empire encompassed all land adjoining the Mediterranean Sea, and it had held on to it for almost one hundred years. Heraclius defeated Persia, the only other major power in the region. Constantinople and Alexandria excelled as centers for learning and art. Byzantine merchants did business from India to France. While Heraclius was able to restore much of the Byzantine Empire, wars with the Sasanian Empire and Muslim armies, and his failure to settle religious disputes within Christianity, left him weakened and contributed to the loss of several of his provinces.[7]

Contributing to Byzantium's decline was what we might today call "mob politics," an appropriate label for much of what describes modern America. Mob politics then, as it has now, replaced serious debate aimed at discovering what is true and finding solutions to challenging problems. The mob politics of the Byzantine era involved something called the circus factions, which were basically composed of fans of various chariot race teams. Recall the chariot race scene in the film *Ben-Hur*, with the partisans in the Roman crowd cheering their favorite driver or jeering the others, and you get a sense of what the circus factions looked like, except these partisans had strong political overtones and affiliations.

The fact that these mobs possessed real political power did not aid in good governance. Imagine if the fans at an NFL football game were making national defense decisions in their inebriated state, let alone lacking any sort of qualifications. That's what the circus factions were. If you think modern American political discourse is corrupt, imagine political and military decisions being made by fans at a sporting event after they have consumed several nine-dollar beers. The Hippodrome was the Byzantine Empire's version of the Roman Coliseum, but without the gladiators. It came to symbolize decadence and contributed to Byzantium's downfall, though there were also other factors, as discussed.

The end came slowly but inevitably, and even though the empire continued in some lesser forms for several centuries, for all practical purposes it had lost its vitality somewhere near the beginning of the sixth century. They were right on schedule, according to Sir John Glubb.

WHAT CAN WE LEARN FROM THE BYZANTINES?

What does all of this have to do with our own approaching demise? On the one hand, there's much to admire in how the Byzantine Empire was built around the Christian faith, because it is that faith, when properly observed, that preserves freedom and security as well as equal rights for women, minorities, and the least among us. There is something comforting to most Christians in imagining a world where not only is it acceptable to practice one's faith but also that faith is preferred and defended by the ruling officials. A strong case can be made that when an empire or nation turns against God, it begins on a path of decline from which it is almost impossible to escape.

That is found not only in scriptural history but in virtually all history.

On the other hand, the Byzantine Empire was a theocracy, and history has shown that once a religion is institutionalized and forced upon people, it loses its power and vitality. The challenge for any nation is to allow religion to function freely without giving it "official" status. That was the vision and hope of America's founding fathers, who wanted the state kept out of the church while protecting the "free exercise" of the faith of believers.

The question for America is, and from the start has been, how do people of faith influence their culture without tearing down the wall that our forefathers felt was necessary to prevent our republic from becoming a theocracy? State religions may be popular for those whose religion aligns with the state, but eventually those religions become compromised by the ever-shifting political winds that blow from the left and the right. England is considered officially Christian and even has an official church—the Church of England—but church attendance in England hovers around a tepid 7 percent of the population. Authentic faith, practiced without government assistance but also without government opposition, is an unstoppable force for good that the Bible describes as salt and light. And it is what we choose to do with this salt and light that will or will not extend America's expiration date.

CHAPTER 4

THE ARAB EMPIRE:
Muhammad's Followers

LIE TO A LIAR, FOR LIES ARE HIS COIN; STEAL
FROM A THIEF, FOR THAT IS EASY; LAY A TRAP
FOR A TRICKSTER AND CATCH HIM AT FIRST
ATTEMPT, BUT BEWARE OF AN HONEST MAN.
—*Arab proverb*

Some people think it is unfair to characterize the contemporary Muslim world as violent or radical, and to be fair, the majority of Muslims living today are generally peaceful, law-abiding citizens who care for the same things other people do: family, faith, meaningful employment, and the like. So where does this image of a people bent on conquering and converting the world by force come from? The answer is complex, but a major source of this characterization comes from the Arab Empire.

The Arab Empire began in 632 CE, following the death of the Muslim prophet Muhammad. Under the leadership of a series of caliphs, or Muslim religious and civil rulers, Arab armies spread their faith, creating an empire that stretched from the Atlantic Ocean to the Indus River, encompassing Syria, Egypt, Persia, North Africa, Palestine, Iraq, Armenia, Afghanistan, India, and Spain. And although what was once a great and vast empire eventually declined, as others have before and after them, its religion, Islam, continues to exert itself as the second-largest and fastest-growing religion in many parts of the world. (In London, it was recently reported that the number one choice of names for newborn sons is Muhammad.)

The Arab Empire cannot be separated from Islam, any more than the Byzantine Empire can be separated from Orthodox Christianity. Islam was and remains the defining aspect of Arab culture and shapes their worldview. Islam seeks to establish a unity between faith in the next world and power in this one, although within Islam itself there are many sects and divisions. As with Christianity, those divisions were sometimes the cause of devastating warfare between factions. To understand the Arab Empire, you have to understand Islam. So before we proceed with the history of the Arab Empire, allow me to offer you a brief description.

A BASIC INTRODUCTION TO ISLAM

Islam is a strictly monotheistic religion, recognizing only one God: Allah. Allah is one person and one substance, as opposed to the Christian God, who is revealed in Scripture as the Trinity, in which there is one God expressed in three distinct personalities: God the Father, God's Son Jesus, and God's Holy Spirit. Many Muslims consider Christianity blasphemy because it worships "more than one god."

The Koran is believed by Muslims to be the verbatim word of Allah and to have existed unaltered throughout eternity in heaven. It cannot be translated into other languages. The English version of the Koran is not called the Koran; it's called *The Meaning of the Glorious Koran*. The duty Allah requires of man is to submit with his entire soul and mind to Allah. Islam is a works-based religion, meaning that humans are born basically good, and as long as we obey Allah's commandments and sincerely repent of our sin, Allah will be merciful and grant us entry into paradise. However, unlike Christianity, in Islam there is no atonement necessary for the expiation of sin. Islam does not require a Savior to suffer the holy wrath of God for the redemption of humans. Allah does not demand the sanctification of his followers. He simply forgives them.

The life of the Muslim is made up of five pillars.

1. profession of faith—Shahada
2. daily prayers—Salat
3. almsgiving—Zakat
4. fasting during Ramadan—Sawm
5. pilgrimage to Mecca—Hajj

Muslims are expected to follow the first four pillars their entire lives and make at least one pilgrimage to Mecca during their lifetime if possible. While these five pillars might be seen as benign and even admirable, they stand in stark contrast to the requirements of the Christian faith: belief in Jesus as the Son of God and repentance from sins to receive the free gift of salvation.

Here's where it gets a little dicey. Observant Muslims point to the liberalization within their own faith—women abandoning the burqa and even the hijab, the use of alcohol, infrequent prayer—warning that it compromises their influence. Similarly, they contend that the secularization of Christianity (to the point where its followers are no different from America's happy pagans) confirms its illegitimacy. While I don't agree with that perspective, I sometimes wonder if postmodern Christianity has inadvertently turned the faith into a social club, while its more conservative counterparts have morphed it into an ad hoc political movement. I'm not suggesting that Christians either return to the legalism of our past, which turned Christianity into a list of dos and don'ts, or abstain from the political process (see Ed Dobson's and my 1999 book *Blinded by Might: Why the Religious Right Can't Save America*). I'm suggesting only that how we live out our faith matters. If there is any hope for our nation to retain its greatness (and we need to define what greatness means), people who are serious and committed followers of Jesus of Nazareth must lead the way by obeying his commands and practicing his teachings consistently and joyfully.

THE AGES OF PIONEERS AND CONQUESTS

Achieving any goal requires three things: inspiration, followed by motivation, and then perspiration. These qualities can be used to achieve bad goals as well as good ones. The expansion of Arab and Muslim influence into an empire contained all three of these qualities.

Following the death of Muhammad, Muslims were without a leader, since a prophet could have no successor. Instead, as I mentioned, Arab leadership depended on caliphs, men who were Muhammad's most loyal followers.

From the start, Arabic Islam used earthly power to achieve what adherents believed to be heavenly goals. Muslim tribes raided villages, seeking to impose their faith and will. They lacked a regular army at first, but that was soon to change. Adherents were rapidly added, sometimes by conversion (a lot of it forced) and other times by means of the sword. A newly organized Muslim navy wiped out the Christian fleet in the Battle of the Masts (655 CE). The expanding Muslim army attacked Constantinople during this period but never succeeded in capturing it.

The rapid military successes were partly a result of the weakness of the conquered countries, brought on by decades of external conflicts and internal structures. (Infighting has been a problem for Islam too, as Sunni and Shia Muslims continue to battle each other today. But both hate the Sufis, whom they regard as heretics, and all branches of Islam—to one extent or another, with a few exceptions—hate Jews and Christians, the latter of whom they call cross worshipers, or polytheists for believing in a triune God.)

At the conclusion of the first Muslim campaign into Spain (711–13 CE), the entire Northwest corner of the Iberian Peninsula was placed under Arab rule. It is one reason some Muslims today continue to regard Spain, beginning with Gibraltar, as still belonging to them, because according to their worldview, once a nation becomes Islamic, it remains Islamic, no matter how long it may be under the control of people they regard as infidels.

The expansion of the Arab Empire cannot be discussed without telling the story of the Battle of Tours in 732 CE, one of the most important battles in history, one that precipitated the decline of the empire. Some historians believe we might all be speaking Arabic if Charles Martel, the de facto ruler of the Frankish kingdoms, had lost that war. It was Martel who repelled Muslim invaders from Spain. That was important because Martel's victory over forces of the emir of Cordoba preserved Western Europe from Muslim conquest and Islamization. But again, note how the Arab Empire relied on force to advance its Muslim faith. It's one thing to desire that others share your beliefs; it's quite another to go and make disciples by holding a sword over their heads.[1]

Why is it important to understand how the Arab Empire used force to gain converts and the territories where these converts lived? It's because modern jihadis remember this history and are resurrecting it and attempting to replicate it in modern times (with less success, as the scattering of ISIS forces in Syria has shown, though terrorism continues). We see them as barbaric and cruel, but they see themselves as preserving their faith. They never give up, mostly because they are religiously motivated. Infidel diplomats from the hated West are not about to dissuade them from what they believe to be a command from their God to conquer the world by whatever means necessary, including lies, subterfuge, coercion, and force. This is what the increasingly secular West fails or, to be more accurate, refuses to understand. By contrast, followers of Jesus are called to attract the lost to their faith through other means: "love, joy, peace, forbearance, kindness, goodness, faithfulness, gentleness and self-control" (Gal. 5:22–23). We are to be known to others by the way we love one another.

THE AGE OF COMMERCE

If you ever travel to an Arab country—or even the Arab Quarter in Jerusalem's Old City—you can experience the bargaining theatrics you won't see in an American or European shopping mall. It is a game Arabs expect you to play. They give you a price of an item you seem interested in, and you counter with a lower price. The merchant feigns offense but after a short time comes back with a price closer to yours. If you shake your head and begin to walk away, he follows you and pleads with you to come back, sometimes asking, "How much do you want to pay?" and the haggling begins again. Finally, you and he agree on a price, and he sells you the item. He smiles. You smile. Each feels satisfied.

This is a scenario in which I have engaged over several years and in many countries. It is fun, and it reveals something about Arab culture and history.

As in other areas, Arabs pioneered development of a vibrant commerce and trade, beginning in the Byzantine and early Islamic Middle East. They established trade networks that were precursors to modern delivery systems, such as the postal service, UPS, FedEx, and Amazon. These trade networks extended over several continents and bodies of water. While the best known of them ran between Europe and Asia, such as the Silk Road, equally important were the overland routes that ran north-south across the Arabian Peninsula to East Africa.

In addition to the obvious commercial benefits, these routes also provided opportunities for cultural exchange that included such diverse peoples as mercenaries, merchants, nomads, and pilgrims.[2] What astounds many historians and even casual observers is how magnificent the Arab Empire once was, in contrast to what much of it is now.

THE AGE OF INTELLECT

The empire reached its zenith under the leadership of a caliph known as Jaffar al-Mansour, who founded and then oversaw the building of the then-great city of Baghdad, which he initially called Madinat as-Salaam, or "the City of Peace." Under his guidance, Baghdad grew into a shining example of the best of Islam. The city attracted scholars from all over the world, largely because of Muslim teaching that "the ink of the scholar is more holy than the blood of the martyr."[3] Because education is so important to Islam, literacy soared in Baghdad, as did the production of books and great poetry and literature. Even the city's remoteness was intentional, as al-Mansour wanted to avoid the factions that were already dividing Islam. As *New Yorker* staff writer Ian Frazier observed, "While Europe still moiled in its Dark Ages, Baghdad was a city of booksellers, bathhouses, gardens, game parks, libraries."[4]

Those unfamiliar with the history of Arab culture may not be aware of that culture's contributions to science and other disciplines. Some historians point to the great centers of learning in Baghdad, Damascus, and Cairo as models for the great universities in the Western world. The caliph Harun al-Rashid sought out intellectuals and scholars from other countries to come to Baghdad and learn from each other. His son, al-Mamun, established the House of Wisdom to translate great literature of the Greeks into Arabic. He invited persons from different countries with various backgrounds for dialogue and mutual learning.

Muhammad al-Khwarizmi was one of the first directors of the House of Wisdom in Baghdad. His major contribution was overseeing the translation into Arabic of the astronomy and mathematical works of Greeks and Indians. His original work had a lasting influence as Islam spread throughout the world. European mathematics also benefited from his intellect.

The word algorithm, which has become more familiar in the age of social media because of the way political and consumer ads are promoted, derived from the Latinization of his name. The word algebra came from the Latinization of *al-jabr*, which is a part of the title of his most famous book. In that book, al-Khwarizmi introduced basic algebraic methods and ways to solve equations. As one who barely got through algebra in high school, I am impressed by his knowledge.

The Middle Ages (also known as the Dark Ages) are thought by most Westerners to be devoid of anything worthy of modern attention. And yet Muslims created a society that was the scientific center of the world. Like Greek and Latin before them, the Arabic language was synonymous with unprecedented learning and science for a period often referred to as a golden age.

Dr. Jamil Ragep, a professor of the history of science at the University of Oklahoma, was quoted in the *New York Times* as saying, "Nothing in Europe could hold a candle to what was going on in the Islamic world until about 1600."[5]

Many historians believe that had it not been for this rise in Arab intellectualism, the Renaissance and the Enlightenment, as well as the Scientific Revolution, might never have occurred. The reason we don't know more about this era is that most of the scientific works have not been translated from Arabic, and that is a shame. Perhaps these works might inspire modern Arabs and Muslims to return to such pursuits and reject the call to terrorism, the elimination of Israel, and the suppression of women, among other deformities.

The contrast with modern Arab/Muslim nations could not be more stark. Despite trillions of dollars in oil money, provided mostly by Western countries, the Arabs have done little to elevate their people to economic independence and to a faith that once encouraged intellectual pursuits. The Koran commands believers to seek knowledge, so in a way many modern practicing Muslims are in rebellion.

THE DECLINE OF THE ANCIENT ARAB EMPIRE

What went wrong? Why did such intellectual pursuits and successes not inspire future generations of Arabs and Muslims? In part, it is because of the profile of most nations—with the West being a notable exception for the moment—which at some point run out of steam and turn inward. Whereas the Arab world once welcomed interaction and cooperation with others, it began to isolate itself. As historian Hillel Ofek observed, "The civilization that had produced cities, libraries, and observatories and opened itself to the world had now regressed and become closed, resentful, violent, and hostile to discourse and innovation."[6] Ofek also identified a rejection of reason and philosophy as contributing to the fall of the Arab Empire. In essence, both were deemed incompatible with Islamic teaching.

Proof that some things never change when it comes to governments and taxes is what happened to the Umayyad Dynasty and its leaders. This Arab dynasty collapsed over the issue of taxes. In essence, the haves were required to pay lower taxes than the have-nots. Since minority non-Muslims paid higher taxes than both, Muslim powers were forced to halt conversions in order to feed their greed for more money. Resentment led to rebellion, marking the beginning of the end of the empire.

WHAT CAN WE LEARN FROM THE ARABS?

As we consider the rise and fall of the Arab Empire, what can we take from them and apply to our own experience? It's difficult for many of us to imagine a robust and almost cosmopolitan Arab world, because its current manifestation appears to be isolated, rigid, and secretive.

Contemporary Muslims in strict Islamic states have been told by many of their clerics to pay attention to what those clerics tell them and not to question or doubt, lest they put their souls in danger of damnation. This is not unique to Islam. Prior to the Reformation, the Roman Catholic Church told its members not to read Scripture and that priests would tell them what they needed to know. It wasn't until Vatican II that this policy was reversed and Catholics were allowed, even encouraged, to read the Scriptures.

The obvious difference is that whereas Catholicism, and Christianity in general, was modernizing, Islam was reverting to its ancient roots. We will soon see whether the initial reforms in Saudi Arabia (such as now allowing women to drive cars) endure. Reforms within Islam can be costly. Some Palestinians who have favored making peace with Israel have paid with their lives. So did Egyptian president Anwar Sadat for his peace treaty with Israel.

America is questioning its own commitment to cooperation with other nations, and in many cases for good reason. Cooperation has not always been reciprocal, especially when it comes to trade policies. The Christian faith, however, has always been at its best when its adherents understand that their true citizenship lies in a kingdom that welcomes anyone regardless of color, ethnicity, or economic status. Perhaps it is from this posture that we can influence our nation to reject the regression and oppression that led to the decline of the Arab Empire.

We don't have any other choice.

CHAPTER 5

THE SPANISH EMPIRE:
How the Mighty Doth Fall

Now we come to one of the largest empires in history, a vast kingdom that in its heyday included parts of the New World, Europe, Africa, and Oceania. Considered by many historians to be the most powerful empire during the sixteenth and seventeenth centuries, almost continually at war someplace in the world, Spain financed many of its conquests with gold from American mines. Today, though a member of the European Union, Spain is no longer an empire but a mere nation struggling to contend with unemployment, one of the lower per capita incomes of all European nations, political extremism, and separatism.

My, how the mighty doth fall.

THE AGE OF PIONEERS

Italy had its artists, but Spain had explorers, some of whom were Italian by birth but came to serve the Spanish Empire. And what brave men they were. Anyone who has studied world—or even American—history knows their names. Their exploits reached to California in the west and Florida in the east of what became the United States.

By far, the most famous of these explorers was Christopher Columbus, the "discoverer" of America. For years, schoolchildren learned the poem

> In fourteen hundred ninety-two,
> Columbus sailed the ocean blue.

Though born an Italian, Columbus undertook all his missions for Spain. America has long honored him with his own holiday in October, though now many calendars are labeling it Indigenous Peoples' Day. Try rhyming that one.

The Portuguese rivaled the Spaniards in their exploratory journeys, but Spain can take credit for the most famous of them. In addition to Columbus, the explorers included Amerigo Vespucci, who was Italian born but became a naturalized Spaniard. Vespucci's maiden voyage began on May 10, 1497. A month later, he reached the Guiana mainland. It was for him that America was named.

Vasco Núñez de Balboa achieved fame for being the first explorer to see the Pacific Ocean from its eastern shore. A park in San Diego is named after him, not to mention the movie prizefighter played by Sylvester Stallone, Rocky Balboa. Okay, those probably have no connection, but I'm trying to be culturally relevant.

Juan Ponce de León achieved fame as the explorer who searched for the fountain of youth. Instead he was the first European to set foot in Florida, which has become anything but a fountain of youth; rather it's the preferred home of many retirees. The state has a town and a park named for him, and at least two cities claim to possess the true fountain of youth. Florida's demographics indicate neither is working.

What motivated these and other Spanish explorers? One could lose one's life in uncharted waters on the open seas. Many did. Ships sank in storms, often taking their crew and valuables to the bottom of the ocean.

In addition to whatever else they were searching for in a world not yet fully known to them, they sought gold, silver, and spices.

CAMEO: *Ferdinand Magellan (1480–1521)*

What schoolchild studying world history has not heard of Ferdinand Magellan? Okay, maybe not modern kids in public schools that teach things much different from what I learned when I was growing up.

Magellan was among the great explorers of Spain (and Portugal). Others included Bartholomew Diaz, who rounded the Cape of Good Hope, Vasco da Gama, who traveled to India, and the most famous of all, Christopher Columbus.

Magellan is credited with becoming the first European to circumnavigate the world, though many of his crew were killed in the Philippines by inhabitants of the island of Mactan, who rebelled against attempts to convert them to Christianity. Magellan took a group of sixty men to attack Mactan (not exactly a good way to win converts), but they were met by fifteen hundred armed Mactan tribesmen. The survivors retreated and, though their ship had been damaged, continued on their way, finally reaching Spain on September 6, 1522.[1]

Magellan was Portuguese. He was born of noble blood in 1480 and as a young boy worked in the queen's household. Upon hearing of the exploits of other Spanish and Portuguese explorers, Magellan also caught the bug and boldly set out to discover places where no European had gone before. Finding a way to get to the Pacific Ocean by ship without having to traverse land masses was considered at the time to be a significant challenge.

Writing for *Smithsonian.com*, Haley Crum picks up the Magellan saga.

> Portugal and Spain were not only competing for dominance in the spice industry, but also for influence in colonies around the world. King Manoel of Portugal was becoming increasingly frustrated with Spain's growing power in the East, especially in the Moluccas, commonly known as the Spice Islands, and was furious when

Magellan pledged his allegiance to Spain and offered its king, Charles V, his plan to find an alternate route to India. This route would enable ships to pass from the Atlantic to the already discovered South Sea through South America.

Magellan had already sailed in the name of Portugal several times, but King Manoel had refused to compensate him when pirates looted his ship. Later, Magellan had fought in North Africa in the name of his homeland but was still not paid.

Once Magellan persuaded King Charles to support his plan, Magellan took an oath of allegiance to Spain, breaking his promise to Portugal. "He couldn't go back to Portugal because he would be executed," writes [historian Helen Nadar of the University of Arizona]. "This was regarded as complete treason, perhaps more so because of the huge rivalry between Spain and Portugal at the time."[2]

Magellan's legacy is summed up in this *Encyclopaedia Britannica* entry: "The Strait of Magellan, off the southern coast of South America, became an important navigational route. His discovery of the trade winds ranks among his most useful and major findings. The expedition gave Europeans a much better understanding of the extent of the earth's size. Much of what we know of Magellan's journey came from Antonio Pigafetta. A crew member of the famed voyage, Pigafetta kept a firsthand account of the voyage. He and his story survived the journey around the globe, and his account later was translated. Magellan had set out with a goal to discover a Western sea route to the Spice Islands. What he helped prove, however, is that the world is indeed round, and much bigger than Europeans previously imagined."[3]

Their successful exploits encouraged English explorers to follow them, but it was the Spanish adventurers who, in addition to seeking things of temporal value, also sought to spread the Christian faith, bringing Catholicism to the New World as a foundation for their expanding empire. Exporting the faith was perhaps their biggest motivation.

There were still people who clung to the view that the world was flat. It was these Spanish explorers, most notably Columbus, who would disabuse them of that belief. Columbus knew he could get to India by sailing east, but since he believed the world was round, he also believed he could get there by sailing west. Oops!

It's difficult to select a starting date for some empires, but the year 1469 for Spain is as good as any. That year, Princess Isabella of Castile married Ferdinand of Aragon. Shortly thereafter the Spanish Empire began to expand. Ferdinand and Isabella decided to finance Columbus's trip to find a new trade route to India. Instead, heading west, he reached Watling Island in the Bahamas and later that month continued on to Cuba, which he thought was mainland China. (No GPS in those days.) Two years later, Ferdinand and Isabella claimed all the lands then referred to as the New World for Spain. It was quite an accomplishment by any standard, but especially in the late fifteenth century.

In addition to bringing back valuables with them, the Spanish explorers opened new sea lanes and new lands, which were, long-term, of greater value. They also brought things to these new lands. These included new languages, literature, music, geography, and cartography.

A blot on the empire's historical reputation is what came to be known as the Spanish Inquisition. To be Spanish meant being Catholic, and so a kind of purge (what today might be called ethnic cleansing) began. Even as Columbus embarked on his voluntary and state-supported first journey in 1492, Jews were being expelled from Spain, as were the Moors. The Spanish Inquisition grew out of a desire to ensure that those residing in Spain were faithful Catholics and not closet Jews or Muslims. Historians Palmer, Colton, and Kramer put it like this: "Life in Spain remained a great crusade, a crusade against Moriscos and Marranos, a crusade carried against the Moors into Africa itself. . . . The crusade crossed the ocean into the Americas. . . . And it was soon to spread to Europe also [to fight Protestants]."[4]

THE AGE OF CONQUESTS

The political maneuvering that took place in Spain to forge a new superpower almost overnight was accomplished not by a Spaniard but by an Austrian. Maximilian I was the Holy Roman emperor. He used the weapon of marriages to unite the Netherlands and Burgundy under his rule. Maximilian then married his son Philip to Joanna, daughter of Ferdinand and Isabella of Spain. Maximilian's grandson Charles V (Charles I in Spain), son of Philip and Joanna, would unite the Holy Roman Empire, the Netherlands, Castile, Aragon, Spanish America, and a sizable chunk of Italy under a single ruler. After Charles V's abdication, two strands of the Habsburg Dynasty would emerge. One ruled in a weakened Holy Roman Empire, the other in a powerful and independent Spanish Empire.

During the sixteenth century, the Spanish fought many wars to gain control of large parts of the Americas, the Pacific, and Europe. In the Americas, there were the Spanish conquests of the Aztec Empire, Guatemala, the Inca Empire, and the Muisca Federation (google that one if you are not a historian). There was also the Philippine-Italian War of 1499–1504. All this gobbling up of territory eventually and inevitably produced political indigestion for the conquerors as well as the conquered.

In the New World, a handful of Spanish conquistadors were able to wipe out several existing empires, primarily by allying with the enemies of the Aztecs and Incas, using superior military technology, and exploiting the massive death rate of the local population, caused by new diseases. The stories of Cortez, Pizarro, and others are well known, but in retrospect there doesn't seem to be much glory in their conquests. The Spanish were not kind rulers, and the increasing knowledge of their activities has even resulted in the rejection of Columbus Day. The Spanish did, however, contribute heavily to the Christian victory at Lepanto in 1571. This battle is widely considered to be one of the most decisive in military history. The Ottoman fleet was utterly destroyed, and although it was quickly rebuilt, the breathing room gained allowed the Spanish to leap ahead in naval technology (driven by their global exploration) and negate the naval threat of the Ottomans. The Ottomans were then forced to wage costly land wars to attempt continual expansion.[5]

In Europe, the Spanish fought constant wars against their traditional opponents (France, England, the Italian city-states). This was all financed by gold from the New World, which triggered massive economic activity before an equally massive crash.[6]

THE AGE OF COMMERCE AND AFFLUENCE

Remember President Obama's stimulus program, which was supposed to produce shovel-ready jobs and revive a moribund economy when it was passed by a Democratic Congress in 2009? The economic rise of Spain was, more than anything, the result of a sixteenth-century equivalent of Obama's stimulus. Literally, there is nothing new under the sun. Everything we think of as an original idea has been tried before, by one person or another, by one country or another, or in one century or another. This is why it is critical we learn from history so as not to repeat the mistakes of the past, though we so often do.

Spanish conquests in the New World had yielded mines rich in silver and gold. Imagine how today's cable TV commercials hawking gold and silver would have played five hundred years ago! Every year, a treasure fleet would arrive in Spain, bringing with it vast stores of wealth. This wealth, for a short time, underwrote the cost of wars, which were necessary to conquer new lands, subdue the population, and keep territories already under Spanish control. Add to those expenses the construction costs associated with massive palaces and cathedrals, subsidies for the arts, and every other type of luxury the nobility desired, and as the late US senator Everett Dirksen (a Republican from Illinois) remarked, "Pretty soon you're talking about real money."[7] Wars are expensive. Depending on who is counting, up to 20 percent of Spain's income every year was spent on warfare.

The Spanish nobility managed to avoid high taxes. Today we might call the ability to avoid taxes loopholes, but unlike today, the poor paid most of the taxes, which is hard to fathom, given their lack of wealth. As one might expect, those paying the most in taxes became bitter against those who paid less or none at all.

Instead of paying much of their wealth to the government, Spanish nobility spent their money on the arts. Call it their version of today's National Endowment for the Arts, except in modern times, taxpayer dollars underwrite the arts, less so individual contributions (though you wouldn't know it watching public broadcasting).

Chris Plante is a conservative talk show host based in Washington, DC. His program is syndicated and can also be heard on the internet through *WMAL.com* from 9:00 a.m. until noon Eastern Time each day. One of his funnier lines is what he says about National Public Radio (NPR), which he calls "national panhandler radio" because they and their sister TV network (PBS) always seem to be begging for money from listeners and viewers.

While one can legitimately quibble about the unfairness of taxation in Spain, the contributions to the arts by Spanish nobility produced some of the world's greatest painters and structures. They include:

- El Greco
- Diego Velázquez
- Francisco de Zurbarán
- Bartolomé Esteban Murillo
- Palace of Charles V
- El Escorial
- Plaza Mayor in Madrid
- Granada Cathedral
- Cathedral of Valladolid

In literature also, Spain produced Cervantes and *Don Quixote*, which contributed more than great love affairs and the song "The Impossible Dream" from the Broadway show *Man of La Mancha*. It is not an exaggeration to call this Cervantes novel one of the most influential works of literature in Spanish history.

Lest we forget, however, these accomplishments in the arts were made possible by what we now call government funding. The pattern was the same then as it is today. When government spends more than it takes in, economic distress occurs, often followed by collapse. In our day, the US has been borrowing from China, mostly, and other nations to ward off the day of reckoning. It's only a matter of time before the debt limit can be raised no more and the economy atrophies, if it does not collapse outright, with possibly a depression worse than that of the 1930s. While we have a national debt of $22 trillion (as of 2018), the Left wants to spend trillions more.

Don't think a depression could happen again? That's what many believed until October of 1929, when the party that was the Roaring Twenties abruptly ended.

In Spain, with the nobles seemingly offended by the notion they should pay taxes—reminiscent of the late hotelier Leona Helmsley's infamous line "Only the little people pay taxes"— stimulus spending by the government contributed to massive inflation, leading to a rapid decline in the value of silver and gold.

It is a history lesson that should keep individuals from being seduced by those gold and silver TV ads. Remember, you are buying at today's higher prices and counting on the value of these and other precious metals to rise. The sixteenth-century Spanish government rolled the dice and lost. I guess the warning "What goes up must come down" wasn't available to them in their day, but if they had studied history—not to mention human nature—they might not have doomed themselves to repeat it.

Eventually, a new trade system was established, with the despicable practice of slavery at its core. Merchants would take slaves from Africa to the New World to trade them for rum, sugar, gold, and silver. Then they took those goods and sold them in Spain for goods to trade in Africa for more slaves. This returned some stability to the Spanish economy, although it was never able to produce such advances in wealth as had the early treasure fleets. Any economy built on the dehumanization of others deserves to collapse.

This economic turmoil corresponded with a period of decline that began almost immediately after the great achievements of Philip II.

Culture

I love definitions because they help focus the mind. For decades, we are said to have been in a culture war. As in any war, it helps to know one's enemy.

One online dictionary defines *culture* this way: "the quality in a person or society that arises from a concern for what is regarded as excellent in arts, letters, manners, scholarly pursuits, etc."[8]

One secondary definition is under the subheading *anthropology*: "the sum total of ways of living built up by a group of human beings and transmitted from one generation to another."[9]

I especially like that second definition.

So culture is a sum total. It is also about ways of living by more than a few humans, with all of that being willed to succeeding generations.

Those of a certain age remember what their parents or grandparents transmitted to them following the Great Depression and World War II. It was the sum total of values and beliefs they shared, the values held by those Tom Brokaw correctly labeled the greatest generation.

Yes, they were imperfect, just as we are, sinners incapable of saving themselves apart from God's mercy and grace. But they saved a nation—several nations—because they embodied the things that mattered most in life: duty, honor, and country. They not only wanted to restore such things to Europe and preserve them for America but also sought to pass these down to their children and grandchildren. They had learned them from *their* parents. It is why they went to war, and although thousands did not come back, their values remained, at least until the self-indulgent 1960s and the generation that followed (as critiqued in my 1994 book, *The Things That Matter Most*).

Today that clash of their culture with ours is stark. My grandmother once admonished me for using words she said nice young men don't say in public. The words that offended her were *toilet paper*. Imagine what this woman, born in 1888, would think of the words heard on TV, in movies, and on the streets today.

Return to the definition given earlier and particularly notice the words *built up*. This suggests to me that the way to change a culture is not from the top down but from the bottom up, not through Washington but through the human heart and individual choices.

It might be too late for that, but it is not too late to make choices for ourselves and for our families, especially where we send our young children to school. It amazes me that so many parents—conservative and Christian parents—see no problem in sending their children to state schools, where they learn they evolved from slime and the reason they like bananas on their cereal is that their nearest relative is at the zoo.

Okay, I exaggerate, but not by much. If your child is a soldier, would you be okay if he or she were trained in a country that was the enemy of the United States? Doesn't the question answer itself? Why, then, would you knowingly and willingly send your child to a school—and then a university—that undermines the values, beliefs, and faith you have tried to teach them?

Don't answer that you want them to be ambassadors for God. I have met many ambassadors, and none are eight-year-olds. Children, like soldiers, must be trained and indoctrinated with the knowledge and principles of the nation (or kingdom) they are expected to serve. Look up two words in a concordance. They are *teach* and *learn*. The verses in Scripture that include these words instruct godly parents in what God expects when it comes to children on loan to us for a brief time.

Legions of young men and women taught such things will build up a culture and ultimately a nation. It is the only way to win a culture war.

The Spanish desire to crush Protestantism wherever possible resulted in open revolt in the Netherlands in 1566. The conflict continued for decades, resulting in a vast expenditure of monetary and human resources. The conflict involved other nations as well, with Protestant England lending aid to the Dutch Protestants. The conflict was global in nature, with English pirates raiding Spanish treasure ships and colonies in the New World. The enormous cost of war on a global scale devastated the Spanish economy through taxation and inflation.

Spain did not emulate England and some of the other empires when it came to an age of intellect. The nobles instead poured themselves into other pursuits, such as the arts.

CRISIS AND DECLINE FOR THE SPANISH EMPIRE

Philip III halted the campaigns against the Dutch and cut back Spain's other foreign ventures. In 1609, he expelled 250,000 Moriscos (Christianized Moors), depopulating the country and causing further damage to the economy. Philip IV, who ascended to the throne after his father's death in 1621, preferred culture to politics.

Spain's golden age reached its height during his reign. He allowed Gaspar de Guzmán, Conde de Olivares, to run the government. Olivares sought to restore and even expand Spanish power abroad. He resumed the Dutch conflict and involved Spain in the Thirty Years' War (1618–1648), which in turn led to war with France after 1635. At first generally successful abroad, Spain's military effort could no longer be sustained at home. Olivares' efforts to increase taxation and conscription led to revolt in 1640, first in Catalonia and then in Portugal. With the home front in chaos, Spain also began to fail abroad. Olivares was ousted, but the wars and revolutions his policies had helped engender haunted Spain for another three decades.

Catalonia was recovered in 1652, but Dutch independence had to be recognized in 1648. Roussillon and Cerdagne were returned to France in 1659, and the independence of Portugal was finally accepted in 1668. Spain was weakened further by the rapid exhaustion of the American silver mines after 1640.[10]

Economically, politically, and even culturally, Spain entered a long period of decline. Its new ruler, Charles II, could not govern effectively, because of physical and mental infirmities. Factional strife characterized Spain at home; lost wars typified it abroad.

At Charles' death, the male line of the Spanish Habsburgs became extinct. Charles willed his throne to his grandnephew, Philip V, duke of Anjou and grandson of the Bourbon king Louis XIV of France, who was the most powerful monarch of his time. Much of Europe viewed the Bourbon acquisition of Spain's still-vast territories with alarm and thus favored the Habsburg claims to the throne, as represented by the younger son of Holy Roman emperor Leopold I. England, the Netherlands, Austria, Prussia, and several smaller countries formed a coalition against Louis XIV. This resulted, in 1701, in the War of the Spanish Succession. In 1711, support of the Habsburg claimant also threatened to upset the European balance of power when, as Charles VI, he became Holy Roman emperor after the death of his brother and inherited the Austrian domains. A compromise was reached in the Treaty of Utrecht (1713), whereby most of Spain's remaining European possessions went to Austria, but the Bourbon claimant was recognized as King Philip V of Spain, and the overseas empire passed intact to him.

After all this turmoil, Spain slowly continued to spiral downward. Adding to its indignity was the loss of its overseas possessions to rebellion. The end finally came, not at the hands of a European power but at the hands of the relatively young American nation. The defeat of the Spanish in the

Spanish-American War saw Spain reduced to a third-rate power, as it remains today.

One might paraphrase a song from the musical *My Fair Lady*: "The reign of Spain now stays mainly in the plain." I know, it's a stretch.

WHAT CAN WE LEARN FROM SPAIN?

In a kind of "those who live by the sword shall also die by the sword" lesson, it is important to note that the Spanish Empire was born out of political maneuvering, and it became irreversibly weakened by political maneuvering in 1713. Spain was not conquered by invaders, nor was Spanish culture absorbed or eliminated. Terrible economic and political management led to military defeat and the defanging of the empire. The important parts of the Spanish Empire were chipped away.

Spain was so consumed by problems that the greater powers that might have invaded ultimately never saw anything worth conquering. How's that for a nation's final epitaph? Nothing worth conquering! It reminds me of a line spoken by Maria in *The Sound of Music*. She said she tried to give her clothes to the poor, but the poor didn't want them.

The content of Glubb's essay that best explains the fall of Spain is "the loss of a sense of duty." Good leaders put factionalism aside for the good of the country. They sacrifice their own property, not to mention their freedom and even their lives, for their country. The nobles of Spain did none of these things. Not wanting to pay taxes is understandable from a strictly human and individualistic point of view, but being unwilling to pay anything to facilitate growth is damning. Spain had everything going for it but blew it. Their death spiral took longer than that of other empires simply because, for one reason or another, no one decided to conquer them.

Could anything be more humiliating?

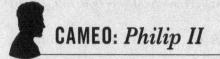

CAMEO: *Philip II*

Philip II (May 21, 1527–September 13, 1598) presided over Spain's golden era, expanding the empire but at tremendous cost. That cost would doom the empire, as it has so many others that have followed similar patterns of behavior.

Not satisfied with the land of Spain, Philip came to dominate Portugal, Naples, and Sicily. He was also known as Lord of the Seventeen Provinces of the Netherlands. His colonial reach extended to the Americas.

He was known in Spain as Felipe el Prudente (Philip the Prudente), and his empire included territories on every continent then known to Europeans, as well as his namesake, the Philippines. The expression "the empire on which the sun never sets" is often associated with Great Britain, but the same could be said of the Spanish Empire.

Philip was a fervent—some would say fanatical—Roman Catholic. He saw himself as a defender of Catholicism in Europe against the Ottoman Turks and the Protestant Reformers, both of which he considered heretics. He limited freedom of worship in the territories over which he was sovereign.

Defeating Protestantism became a top goal. It led to heresy trials, during which hundreds of Protestants were burned at the stake. He intensified the Inquisition and even banned students from studying elsewhere. He also banned books printed outside the kingdom.

Like so many rulers throughout history who attempted to enhance their empires, Philip ignored the costs. Though his treasury took in larger and larger amounts of gold and silver from the mines in America, it was never enough. Sounds like our modern government, which refuses to reduce spending while certain politicians demand even higher taxes on half the nation that earns enough money to pay them. But I digress.

The price of Philip's overreach has been noted by Bernard Moses. In the *Journal of Political Economy*, Moses writes, "Passing over the details of the effects of the colonial system and the transatlantic trade, attention may be directed to the influence of the government on the economic affairs of Spain. It may be noticed, in the first place, that the extensive dominions involving the government in large expenses in carrying on wars into which it was drawn by an aggressive ambition, made a demand on the nation which the public revenue, even when supplemented by the treasures of America, could not satisfy. Through the great undertakings of Charles the Fifth and Philip the Second, the expenditures went on from year to year carrying over an increasing burden upon the income of the future, so that at the death of Philip the Second Spain had a debt of one hundred and forty millions of ducats."[11]

One thousand ducats would be 110.7 ounces of gold. Gold was selling for $1,418.51 per ounce at the end of July 2019. Do the math.

CHAPTER 6

THE OTTOMAN EMPIRE:
Winners and Losers

In the 1950s, a singing group known as the Four Lads had a popular song written by Jimmy Kennedy and Matt Simon. The song reappeared years later in the film *They Might Be Giants*. It's a clever lyric and one that should persuade people with even a modicum of interest in history to probe a little deeper. It's about changing the name from Istanbul to Constantinople. Here is an excerpt.

> Why they changed it I can't say
> People just liked it better that way
> Why did Constantinople get the works?
> That's nobody's business but the Turks.

It may have been nobody's business but the Turks in the 1950s, but today, given the turmoil in the Middle East and the resurgence of militant Islam, it should be everyone's interest in the West.

There is a conceit, especially in the West, that nothing of value emerged from any other culture or civilization before the modern era. Any student of even high school history should know better. The ancient Turks made significant contributions in their arts and especially textiles. Turkish rugs today, as for many centuries before, are highly valued as works of art, as well as practical floor coverings.

Sir John Glubb's pattern states that the average age of an empire is about 250 years. The Ottoman state existed for approximately 600 years. Like the Byzantines (whose empire lasted for 1,000 years), the Ottomans were an empire, as we think of an empire, for only a portion of their existence. In the fifteenth and sixteenth centuries, the Ottoman Empire was one of the most powerful forces, if not the most powerful, on earth. From the seventeenth century until its final dissolution in 1922, the empire shrank because of defeat in war by external enemies and rebellion within. It's an all-too-familiar pattern, as we have repeatedly seen.

THE AGE OF PIONEERS

The Ottomans began as soldiers fighting for Islam against the Byzantine Empire. After centuries of war against the Byzantines, Mongols, and others, a prince known as Osman ruled over a small patch of territory in northwestern Anatolia. The year was 1293. It is here that we will date the start of the Ottoman Empire. From 1293 onward, Osman and his successors rapidly expanded their territory. The disastrous Fourth Crusade had permanently crippled the Byzantine Empire, and the Ottomans took full advantage. They moved to conquer land along the Bosporus Straits. Success in warfare is bound to attract additional support, and the Ottomans found that as they gained victories against the Byzantines and moved past Constantinople (which was still too strong a fortress) and into Europe, they attracted many thousands of supporters from displaced Turkmen. It proved the cliche that nothing succeeds like success. People enjoy being on the side of winners, and the Ottomans knew how to win.

One of the primary leaders in these early years was Murad I. He wisely decided to retain vassals in European territories rather than replace them (a lesson American president George W. Bush failed to learn when American forces displaced Saddam Hussein's party members en masse, creating a leadership vacuum and instability in Iraq). Europeans could keep their territories if they submitted to the Ottoman leader, paid tribute, and provided troops for his army. This has always been a pattern within Islam. Infidels could remain in land conquered by Muslims, but only at a price. In return, the Muslims did not impose occupation forces or administrative bureaucracies on their new subjects. This is not unlike the Persian Empire, discussed earlier.

Despite some setbacks in Anatolia, the Ottomans were in a strong position when a young man named Mehmed II ascended to the throne. Blessed with a powerful state and skilled advisers, he would more than earn his future moniker, the Conqueror.

THE AGE OF CONQUESTS

In 1453, Mehmed II took the city of Constantinople after a two-month siege. The outcome was never in doubt, and the attack had been inevitable. It was impossible for the Ottomans to leave in someone else's hands a city that was important both strategically and culturally. The city was renamed Istanbul, the Hagia Sophia was converted into a mosque, and Mehmed II became the most famous Muslim ruler in the world. Mehmed II would spend most of his time expanding Ottoman territory into Europe and Anatolia. One of his more memorable opponents was the delightfully named Vlad Dracula, prince of Wallachia. In this conflict, Vlad Dracula became a legend after impaling tens of thousands of Turks and leading a night attack on Mehmed II's army in an attempt to kill or capture the sultan. Mehmed II achieved success in the Mediterranean Sea as well, laying the groundwork for the capture of Rhodes and establishing the Ottomans as a great naval power.

At its zenith, the Ottoman Empire dominated most of southeastern Europe, approaching Vienna, Austria. It included present-day Hungary, the Balkan region, Greece, parts of Ukraine, and portions of the Middle East. It also encompassed North Africa, as far west as Algeria, and large portions of the Arabian Peninsula.

THE AGE OF DECADENCE

While the Ottoman Empire at its pinnacle was the superpower of Europe, the Middle East, and North Africa and maintained the infrastructure and educational system necessary to preserve that status, the center of intellectual inquiry and economic activity was beginning to shift rapidly to Western Europe. For a time, there was a shared benefit in all of their economic, intellectual, and cultural achievements. However, the Ottomans would eventually be eclipsed by the Renaissance and the Enlightenment.

After his numerous conquests and with the Ottoman Empire at its peak, Suleyman I retreated from public life to enjoy his harem. The sultan left day-to-day policy and even foreign policy in the hands of his grand vizier. This office was afforded power second only to the sultan, and obedience was expected and given to the vizier. This pattern was certainly followed by Suleyman's successors, and the harems and lust of the Ottoman sultans became legendary. If one travels to Istanbul today, one can see the palace that housed only members of the harem. If you start typing "Ottoman sultan" into Google and scroll down, on the list is "Ottoman sultan harem." It does not take a PhD in social science to know that such lasciviousness will not have a good impact upon the quality of leadership. Decadence has more than one father, but the lust of the flesh is not an uncommon contributor to any empire's decline.

CAMEO: *Suleyman (1494–1566)*

Suleyman (1494–1566) was called magnificent as part of his title, and so he was in his person.

Muslims and Europeans regarded him as the world's most significant ruler, which was no mean feat, given the religious and cultural differences between those peoples. Suleyman, like other Muslim leaders who preceded and followed him, used the military to expand his empire in both easterly and westerly directions. At one time, his expansionist goals threatened to reach the heart of Europe.

Unlike much of the modern Muslim world, Suleyman was behind many cultural and architectural projects. In the mid-sixteenth century, Istanbul was known as the most architecturally energetic and innovative city in the world.

When it comes to good poetry, most people would not cite Islam as on a level with the world's best-known poets, but the poetic writings of Suleyman are considered by those with knowledge of the field to be the best Islam has produced.

Suleyman was a visionary, sponsoring artists, religious thinkers, and philosophers who rivaled the most educated courts with similar artistic and intellectual interests in Europe.

He enjoyed several other monikers which fit his accomplishments. These included the Just, the Lawgiver, the Conqueror, and the Builder. Historian Suzan Yalman of Koc University in Istanbul writes, "Under Süleyman . . . the Ottoman empire reached the apogee of its military and political power. Süleyman's armies conquered Hungary, over which the Ottomans maintained control for over 150 years, and they advanced as far west as Vienna."[1]

There is great debate in modern Turkey as to just how magnificent Suleyman actually was. As the *Economist* has noted, "No matter that he had his own son murdered, among several dastardly deeds. Modern Turks like to boast of his armies reaching the gates of Vienna and to refer to him as the 'lawgiver.' A British historian, Jason Goodwin, writes that Suleyman was 'majestic enough to stock his court with an unusual number of buffoons, dwarves, mutes, astrologers, and silent janissaries' and that he ruled so long 'that he became something of an Ottoman Queen Victoria.'"[2]

Suleyman's remains were discovered in 2015 in Hungary, according to a Hungarian historian.[3]

America, are you paying attention?

The end of the reign of Suleyman I occurred at the end of the sixteenth century. This time period saw a significant shift in the defense establishment of the Ottoman Empire. For most of Ottoman history, as in many cultures, the cavalry was the most important component of the army. As such, the men who formed the heavy cavalry (the nobility) were afforded a large amount of political power. Now, partly because of technological changes and partly because of political realities, that role moved to the janissaries (gun-carrying soldiers) and the rest of the troops associated with the devshirme system, and they assumed dominance.

The devshirme system would be odious to modern people, but in the history of Islam, it was thought to be an important part of their religion. Under devshirme, Christian boys were taken from their families as a tax and educated to serve as bureaucrats and soldiers. These boys were often forcibly converted to Islam and became slaves of the state. As a result of the dominance of the janissaries in the Ottoman army by the end of the sixteenth century, the janissaries became a state within a state. Positions that were once based on merit became subject to corruption and nepotism, contributing to the decline of Ottoman governance.[4]

This political and governmental infighting prevented the Ottomans from adapting to a rapidly changing world. Europeans were taking to the seas to explore the known and especially the unknown world. They were able to bypass old land trade routes to the East that traversed Ottoman territories. Instead they made use of faster and cheaper sea-based trade routes. Without that rich trade, the Ottoman Empire's economy began to suffer. The economic center of power in Europe was moving from what was at one point the Eastern Roman Empire to the new rising global powers of Spain, France, Britain, and the Netherlands. Economic stagnation and the inability to pay the government apparatus led to social unrest. Rebellion, riots, food shortages, and a lack of basic social cohesion were the predictable and inevitable results. A lack of food is bound to cause turmoil. Consider modern-day Venezuela, where it is increasingly difficult to find basic necessities like food and medicine, even toilet paper. A once-rich nation, Venezuela has squandered its assets on a failed political philosophy.

While the army was able to suppress unrest in almost all instances, from the seventeenth century onward, Ottoman military strength began to collapse, weakening in relation to that of the West. This collapse did not occur all at once. Even after the great Christian victory at Lepanto in 1571, the Ottoman navy was rebuilt within two years. However, it became increasingly difficult for the Ottomans to absorb such losses.

Constant warfare with the Habsburg Dynasty, particularly the Austrian branch, took its toll. The turning point in this several-centuries-long struggle was the Siege of Vienna in 1683. Many books and other works have been written on this battle. An Ottoman army numbering in the hundreds of thousands lay siege to the city. A Christian coalition led by the Polish warrior-king John III Sobieski and numbering fewer than ninety thousand broke the siege and routed the Ottoman army. The Christian counterattack involved what very well may be the largest recorded cavalry charge in Western military history. Eighteen thousand Christian cavalry charged downhill into the Ottoman lines. Think of the charge of the Riders of Rohan before the walls of Minas Tirith in part three of the Lord of the Rings, *The Return of the King*.

By the time the nineteenth century arrived, no Western state any longer feared the Ottomans. Their territories were picked off by stronger nations. This earned the Ottoman Empire the name "sick man of Europe." But the empire tried to hold on to what remained, although at this time it could claim control over only a more limited amount of land, which is now called Turkey. The First World War would see the final extinguishing of the Ottoman Empire, and the territory that was not taken by the Allies officially became known as the Republic of Turkey, although now it is less of a republic under President Erdoğan and is increasingly displaying characteristics associated with a dictatorship.

During most of the empire's existence, the official religion was Islam. As the Turks expanded their territory and the influence of Islam into what today is the Middle East, this expansion resulted in what came to be known as the Crusades. There were eight in all, and modern secularists enjoy criticizing Christians for them when Christians warn of the threat of radical Islam, as if to state a moral or religiously motivated equivalency. While the Crusades are admittedly viewed as a scar on the face of the church, most historians agree that the threat of Muslim expansion was real and merited a response, especially given the church's desire to reclaim the Holy Land from Muslim control.[5]

Perhaps, at least in part, because of religious conflict, the Turkish constitution was amended in 1924. The amendment removed the provision declaring that the "religion of the state is Islam." The main leader responsible for turning Turkey away from a theocracy to a more democratic and secular nation was the country's first president, Mustafa Kemal Atatürk. His influence continued long after his death in 1938, but his vision is being replaced, in a throwback to ancient times, by Turkey's current president, Recep Tayyip Erdoğan, who was first elected in 2014 and who survived a coup attempt and a subsequent reelection that some believed was tainted by questionable vote counting. After that election, Erdoğan acted unilaterally to expand his powers.

While Atatürk inaugurated a secular government, he allowed what Americans might call the free expression of religion.

Whether you were a Muslim, a Christian, a Jew, or an atheist, you stood as an equal before the government. That is rapidly changing in our day, as militant Islam under Erdoğan is again rearing its head, and religious pluralism is losing its appeal.

THE DECLINE

When it comes to success, getting there is often easier than staying there.

Empires require energy, money, and sacrifice to create, and it takes those same elements in greater abundance to maintain them. In the case of the Ottoman Empire, creeping fatigue began in the late sixteenth century.

Corruption and nepotism, economic difficulties and social unrest, a weakened central government and military defeats were multiple factors contributing to the decline of the Ottoman Empire. In these, the Turks were little different from empires before or after them. They learned little from history and so were doomed to repeat it.

WHAT CAN WE LEARN FROM THE OTTOMANS?

Despite its decline, a battle continues for the soul of this once-great empire turned run-of-the mill nation. According to a story in the January 2, 2018, issue of the *Irish Times*, an increasing number of Turks want the Hagia Sophia—this mosque-turned-church-turned-museum—to revert to a mosque.[6] Thousands of worshipers have turned up outside the ornate building each May in recent years to observe the Muslim conquest of the city and to rally for the building to be converted once again. Muslims don't forget, believing that any territory or building that was once Muslim remains Muslim no matter what has happened to it in the interim.

Since the AK Party, a party that leans toward a more fundamentalist view of Islam, came to power in 2003, the secular national identity has eroded, and a worldview that reflects an Islamic outlook is gaining strength.

One downside of converting the Hagia Sophia into a mosque is the likely loss of tourism. Millions of tourists visit the Hagia Sophia each year, bringing with them tens of millions of dollars that contribute to the Turkish economy. Turning the museum into a mosque would almost certainly cause significant portions of tourist income, especially that from Western and non-Muslim tourists, to disappear, with potentially disastrous results for businesses and employment.

In addition, the museum's centuries-old mosaics would have to be destroyed or covered up. Turkey has a Christian population of only about 160,000, so most of the calls for preserving the Hagia Sophia as a museum are coming from outside the country. As Turkey grows more Islamic, it is unlikely the government will pay much attention to outside infidels.

Zeki Sakarya, who runs a souvenir crafts store not far from the museum, is quoted in the *Irish Times* story: "The Hagia Sophia as a museum is better; we have enough mosques in Istanbul. It makes no sense to favor one group over another."[7]

That, however, is what fundamentalist Islam does. It favors itself over all other groups, religious and secular. If the Hagia Sophia returns to its earlier status as a mosque, it will be a powerful statement, not only for Turks and Turkey but for much of the rest of the Islamic world, which takes such things as evidence they are obeying the commands of Allah.

It has become popular among Christians to ignore the very real threat of a resurgent militant Muslim movement. Part of the reason for that is an admirable effort to acknowledge that not all Muslims are terrorists and that currently the vast majority of Muslims in America are decent, law-abiding, tax-paying, productive citizens who hold values similar to our own. At the same time, however, a number of Muslims believe that the Koran teaches that their religion should dominate the world, by violent means if necessary.[8]

Should we be alarmed? Yes, but our reaction must be based on love, not fear, as well as confidence in God's kingdom. As Jesus reminds us in the book of John, "Take heart! I have overcome the world" (16:33). Remember, we are citizens of that higher kingdom first, and when we live by that kingdom's values and instructions, we can have a great influence on this temporal nation.

In fact, there are reports of Muslims converting to Christianity in large numbers in places like Afghanistan and Sudan. Erwin Lutzer, pastor of the historic Moody Church, suggests that God has brought Muslims to America for a reason, and that is for them to experience true freedom to choose what and how they believe. "If we approach them with kindness and a willingness to learn about their faith, they will also be more willing to listen to us. It is a privilege to represent Jesus Christ to those who are strangers to our Savior."[9]

For some of us, that response is a tough one to swallow, especially when we read of churches being burned by Muslim militants in Africa and the massacre of Christian families. And yet Christianity has grown to become the largest religion in the world, not by might or power but by individual believers like you and me reflecting the love of Jesus to all, even to our religious and political enemies.

CAMEO: *Sultan Ibrahim I (1615–1648)*

One would be hard-pressed to find someone weirder, more debauched, and more responsible for the moral decline of any empire than Sultan Ibrahim I, one of the most carnal rulers in Ottoman history—and that's saying something.

Infamous for its harem, the palace for concubines still stands in Istanbul along the Bosporus River. It is a magnificent structure, lit at night and impressive from the water. What went on inside and in the sultan's palace (not to mention his mind) is hard to fathom, even in modern "anything goes" cultures.

Dimitrie Cantemir, a Moldavian historian and musician, wrote in his book *The History of the Growth and Decay of the Othman Empire*, first published in 1734, about Ibrahim I's debauchery. He wrote on how the sultan was "exhausted with the frequent repetition of venereal delights," how the sultan demanded a new virgin be brought to him every Friday, and how the sultan would chase the naked women of his harem around while they made noises like stallions.[10]

Of course, such activities dramatically limited his ability to govern his kingdom effectively. You would not expect Hugh Hefner or Charlie Sheen to run an empire; they would be too busy pursuing carnal pleasures.

Ultimately, he was strangled in his own palace in order to remove him from the throne. It was an ignominious end to a life that had an ignominious beginning, with little in between that contributed positively to the empire, much less to the sultan.

CHAPTER 7

THE BRITISH EMPIRE:
Where the Sun Never Sets

THIS BLESSED PLOT, THIS EARTH,
THIS REALM, THIS ENGLAND.
—*from John of Gaunt's speech in*
William Shakespeare's **Richard II**

The English-speaking island north of the European continent has been called many things over the centuries: England, Britain, Great Britain, and in a derivation from Latin, Britannia. Today it is often referred to by the boorish letters UK, for United Kingdom. Imagine Shakespeare writing, "This blessed plot, this realm, this UK." It just doesn't have the same ring to it.

Historians date the birth of the British Empire in different years, even different centuries. Like most empires, Britain had a small and unremarkable start, evolving from overseas possessions and trading posts between the late sixteenth and early eighteenth centuries. By 1913, the empire was at its pinnacle, governing an estimated 412 million people, which was nearly a quarter of the world's population. By 1920, British rule comprised about 24 percent of the earth's landmass. The saying about an empire "on which the sun never sets" was not an overstatement, because the sun always seemed to be shining on one of its territories.

Militarily, geographically, and culturally, Britannia at one time ruled much of the world.

It is somewhat ironic that Queen Elizabeth I—a woman literally in a man's world, given the long line of dominant male kings (in this she was an anomaly, as was Catherine the Great of Russia, who is profiled elsewhere)—is due credit for expanding Britain's reign and rule. In many ways, she had the strength of the Iron Lady, Margaret Thatcher, who as prime minister in the late 1970s and 1980s led a much smaller Britain with similar resolve.

Under the rule of Elizabeth I (1558–1603), a true national identity was born. A powerful example of this can be found in the Spanish invasion of 1588. The invasion was launched by Philip II of Spain in an attempt to overthrow Queen Elizabeth I and restore Catholic rule in England. The plan was to sail a massive fleet from Spain to the Spanish-occupied Netherlands, pick up a battle-hardened Spanish army, and land them in England. On paper, the English had no chance, but after a ferocious naval battle, the English prevented the Spanish fleet from joining up with the Spanish army. During the return to Spain, nature completed the work begun by the English and destroyed much of the Spanish fleet. The defeat of the Spanish in the armada campaign was seen as an act of divine intervention and blessing on England. Even then, "divine intervention" meant that God was on the side of the victorious.

Years of continuous war forced the English to expand their knowledge of the world and their presence within it. Most important, the English would make their presence felt in North America.

As Glubb describes it, this part of the arc of an empire is characterized by the fearlessness and daring of the nation.[1] Inevitably, though, this overreach and the gobbling up of so much land, plus demands upon its residents (notably taxes in

America, which resulted in rebellion and the loss of the Thirteen Colonies), led to the British Empire's decline and fall. Today's England is barely a shadow of its former self. Scotland even attempted to secede from the UK in 2014 through a referendum. Though voters defeated it, separation sentiment remains strong. Older voters mostly want to stay within the UK, while most younger voters want to break with London. Demographics may not work in favor of Scots wishing to remain under the authority of the Crown.

Concerning the first stage of an empire, Glubb writes, "Again and again in history we find a small nation, treated as insignificant by its contemporaries, suddenly emerging from its homeland and overrunning large areas of the world."[2] This rapid emerging is what England did under Elizabeth I. Few believed that this tiny land would, or even could, have such an enormous bearing on European affairs.

Vision is always key to building nations into empires, but when the leader with the vision dies, it is difficult to transfer that vision to others, because their own vision may conflict with that of their predecessor, or worse, they may have no vision at all. As Scripture warns, "Without a vision the people perish" (Prov. 29:18). George H. W. Bush famously disparaged this wisdom as "the vision thing."[3]

By the time Elizabeth I ascended to the throne, the English had lost their last foothold outside of the British Isles. Calais had fallen in 1559. By the time of her death, England's role in the world was rapidly expanding, with a strong and growing presence in North America and the Caribbean. Once the 1700s began, Britain increased its power through large and impressive military victories. By the time Napoleon was defeated for the final time at Waterloo in 1815, England had achieved world dominance, which lasted until the beginning of World War II.

CAMEO: *Stanley Baldwin*

No one person can be credited—or blamed—for the end of the British Empire, but one man was unarguably a contributor to it. He is literally a forgotten man in British history—and probably deserves to be, except as a cautionary tale. His name was Stanley Baldwin, and although he displayed some quirky and even admirable traits, such as donating one-fifth of his family's fortune to help pay down the national debt (a gesture that might have had more meaning had he also been able to constrain spending by Parliament), his negatives far outweighed his positives.

As Martin Kettle wrote about Baldwin in the *Guardian* in 2014, "Although he was prime minister three times in the interwar period— briefly in 1923, more extensively from 1924 to 1929, and then finally from 1935 to 1937—he is always overshadowed by his more dramatic and glamorous contemporaries Lloyd George and Churchill. His most widely remembered achievement, if he still has one, was to drive through the abdication of Edward VIII in 1936. His long-term reputation is still haunted by his failure to stem the rise of Hitler in the 1930s."[4]

Three years after this article appeared, Anne Perkins wrote that there was another side to Baldwin's strength and that his focus was more on popular will (today we might call it an opinion poll or focus group) than on making tough decisions that were best for his country. Like many of his peers (notably Neville Chamberlain), Baldwin was in denial about Britain's need to rearm in the face of Germany's military buildup. While he saw rising storm clouds from the Continent and believed another world war would destroy civilization, he was unwilling to do the necessary things that would prevent it from happening.[5]

Baldwin's denial of what seemed obvious to Churchill (who was obtaining classified documents from the British Foreign Office's Ralph Wigram) was enough to forever taint him in the eyes of the future prime minister.

Some see parallels with at least one American politician. In 2016, President Barack Obama declared, "We are living in the most peaceful, prosperous, and progressive era in human history" and, "The world has never been less violent."

That was true for a time, but Obama was reluctant to confront China, Iran, North Korea, Russia, and the Middle East, instead kicking the can down the road to the Trump administration.

As the *National Review* noted, "Obama is the U.S. version of Stanley Baldwin, the suave, three-time British prime minister of the 1920s and 1930s. Baldwin's last tenure (1935–1937) coincided with the rapid rise of aggressive German, Italian, and Japanese Fascism."[6]

The lesson that can be drawn from Stanley Baldwin's tenure in the British government (and in history) is that unpreparedness serves as a sign to freedom's enemies of an unwillingness to fight to preserve that freedom. Neville Chamberlain—another contributor to Britain's decline as an empire—cared more about preserving an illusory peace than about arming Britain to do the necessary work of defeating evil. In his "Peace in Our Time" declaration following the Munich Pact, Chamberlain followed Baldwin's earlier instincts, which led to disastrous results.

THE AGE OF CONQUESTS

The British Empire's arc from rise to fall is longer than Sir John Glubb's estimate of 250 years, but the trajectory remains the same. From 1700 to 1815, the British Empire found itself in a perpetual state of war. During those 115 years, Britain advanced from a relatively weak nation to become the undisputed master of the sea. While still not the greatest power in Europe, Britain had the greatest influence. It was an age in which alliances were in constant flux. There were, however, two opponents Britain could always count on facing: France and Spain. Britain was by far the greatest victor, on the whole, in the major conflicts of this time period, which began with the War of the Spanish Succession (1702–1715) and continued with the War of the Austrian Succession (1740–1748), the Seven Years' War (1756–1763), and the Napoleonic Wars (1803–1815). More than twenty smaller wars were simultaneously fought by the British, in all corners of the world (with the exception of frigid Antarctica!). While the British did lose some conflicts, their march to victory was relentless and ultimately successful.

It was not only on the battlefield (and at sea) that Britain could claim success. The British also spread colonies and outposts all over the world, in what today might look like a franchise operation worthy of Starbucks and McDonald's, or ubiquitous Chinese restaurants. The two most important examples of this are North America and India. (Africa also became an important addition as the British Empire expanded still farther in the mid-1800s.)

Lessons learned from the British Empire's expansion could be applied today when it comes to the deployment of military force in foreign lands. The British chose to avoid large troop commitments to the European continent proper and instead focused on using their navy to raid enemy coastal strongholds in Europe and blockade enemy ports. This military strategy allowed them to commit larger forces to the colonies in North America and move forces around to aid allies as required.

In addition to achieving military victories and expanding its territory, Britain also began to mature rapidly in technology, finance, and influence. Britain quickly proved its ability to deploy forces effectively in all corners of the globe. British diplomatic skills grew rapidly and, in some circumstances, helped secure advantages without war and conclude peace settlements favorable to the empire. In all of its exploits, Britain never suffered catastrophic losses with any treaty, except the Treaty of Paris of 1783, which recognized American independence.

Perhaps of most importance, the British Empire emerged from this age in a strong economic position, allowing it to fund both the navy and a professional army. Navies are expensive to maintain, but that investment was returned many times when the fleet was called upon to engage in war and to maintain long periods of peace. While the territory Britain controlled had not reached its peak by 1815, the stage was set for the empire to grow virtually anywhere its rulers desired, and there was little that lesser powers could do about it.

THE AGE OF COMMERCE

Economic considerations have long served as motives for an empire's expansion and also have led to their demise. The problem comes when ideology or political goals replace an understanding of human nature. Incentives derive from motivation. If governments tax too much and spend too much, motivation is harmed, and people are less inclined to work hard, because they know significant portions of their profits will be seized by the government. Britain's economic policies following the defeat of Napoleon in 1815 serve as one of many historical examples.

More than twenty years of war had contributed to an enormous debt. At the time of the American Revolution, Britain's debt was nearly 127 million pounds. By 1815, it had soared to more than 900 million pounds. Taxes were raised to help pay down the debt. It didn't work, because high taxes reduce incentive, and the undermining of incentive produces less income and thus less tax revenue.

Writing in *Financial Analysts Journal*, Jude T. Wanniski, a proponent of contemporary supply-side economics, observes,

> What made the Industrial Revolution and the Pax Britannica possible was the audacity of the British Parliament in 1815. Spurred by middle-class agitators . . . the legislature rejected the stern warnings of the fiscal experts and in one swoop eliminated [William] Pitt's income tax, which had been producing 14.6 million pounds, or a fifth of all revenues, and tariffs and domestic taxes that had been producing 4 million pounds more. Had the British left their tax rates high in an attempt to quickly pay down their debts, the 60-year bull market that followed would not have been possible.[7]

It was expanding revenues that produced debt reduction. Britain became the largest creditor nation in the world and had to keep reducing taxes in order to avoid surpluses. Imagine that! Taxes were eventually reimposed, because politicians cannot help themselves.

"Until 1914, the British income tax had been very nearly proportional . . . all income classes paid the same rates. After 1914, the system was progressive. . . . This began the reversal of Britain's course in the nineteenth century. Instead of tax cuts, expansion, revenue increase, tax cuts, etc., the trend in Britain has been tax increase, contraction, revenue decline, tax increase.

Racism

Some have called it America's original sin, though it hasn't always been America's. Britain had a vibrant slave trade—the ultimate and most shameful example of racism—and although it didn't take a civil war in that country to end slavery, the feelings about race and class ran just as deep there as here.

Harvard professor Henry Louis Gates Jr., a friend of mine, has done some excellent work in several series carried on PBS. He has traced the DNA of some prominent African Americans back to slave ancestors, and that of some prominent whites back to their ancestors who were slave owners.

Gates, who is African American, decided to have his own DNA examined, and to his astonishment, he found he is mostly Irish.

When I saw his first series, *African American Lives* (which can still be viewed online at *pbs.org*), the thought occurred that racism is basically a form of self-hatred. We are all mixed up in the great gene pool of life, and there are no purebred humans.

To hate another person because of the color of his or her skin is a sin, pure and simple.

As with other cultural conflicts, too many of us don't know each other. We see ourselves as members of tribes or categories, and we think we know enough about an individual because of their membership in a certain tribe or category.

It works in reverse too. Think about the few politically conservative African Americans you have heard of or possibly know. When notables like Justice Clarence Thomas, perhaps the most famous conservative African American of our time, or Professor Thomas Sowell speak or write, they are often denounced by the liberal establishment as being insufficiently black. This slander says black people and other minorities (and women too, for that matter) should think like a group and not as individuals. It is its own form of racism (and sexism).

Modern society has rightly rejected the bigoted statement "They all look alike," regarding those of other races. But a parallel idea has emerged: that everyone of a particular race should think alike. That's just as racist.

Dr. Martin Luther King Jr. once said that Sunday morning was the most segregated hour of the week in America. He was speaking of church services. That may have been the result of racism and segregation in the past, but today it is a kind of tribalism of our own making. How many white people have visited, much less joined, black churches, or the reverse? Yes, we seem more comfortable with people of our own color and beliefs, but breaking those man-made barriers and getting out of our comfort zones is a first step toward addressing racism.

Question: If you are a white person reading this, have you ever invited people who are of a different race, ethnicity, or nationality for dinner in your home? Would you go to their home? Would you allow your children to become friends with their children?

We don't know each other, and that is an underlying cause of racism and so many other problems that confront us. Hospitality works, if it's genuine. Try it. Such an outreach might change you and your attitude toward people who are different from you, even more than it changes your guests.

Balancing the budget became the process of increasing the 'supertax' on higher incomes."[8] So it is today in the UK, with a progressive income tax *and* a value-added tax of 20 percent on virtually everything, which stifles growth, leads to more dependency on government, and reduces revenue.

At the end of World War II, Winston Churchill and the Tories, who wanted to maintain the increasingly costly colonial empire, were thrown out of office. Just two years later, in 1947, India declared its independence, and the British Empire was effectively over.

THE AGE OF AFFLUENCE

Roughly paralleling what Mark Twain labeled the Gilded Age in America was Britain's Victorian era.[9] The British economy began to expand in the mid-1800s, when there was a dramatic policy shift from protectionism to free trade. Yes, it would for a time leave behind a significant portion of the population, but it set the stage for the era that followed, an era that lifted many boats and created a vibrant British middle class, as happened in America.

Heavy foreign investment also contributed to reshaping the British economy, as did the growth of manufacturing, an increase in small businesses, and the proliferation of banks, insurance companies, shipping, and railways—the sorts of things that fuel economic growth.

While the 1930s presented hardships for many Britons, those who had or could find jobs benefited from depressed prices, which contributed to their affluence. If you paid little for the basics of life, you had more to spend on other things, such as a nicer house, better clothes, travel, and even a modern automobile.[10]

After the end of World War II, Britain began a slow recovery from the general economic struggles of that period. It began to face a far subtler danger than the Luftwaffe's bombing of London. Dr. Martha Kirby, a postgraduate researcher at the University of Glasgow, describes a resurgent economy that led to "the freedom to indulge in consumerism as never before." According to Kirby, one of the significant results of this new prosperity was a "rising tide of obesity."[11]

If being obese is a sign of prosperity, why do we see so many weight loss ads on TV in Britain and America? Just asking.

Who could blame Britain—or America—for wanting more after suffering the double blow of the Great Depression and

World War II? But just as a balanced diet is essential to good health, so too is a balanced outlook toward possessions. The Puritan ethic of living within one's means was in many cases thrown to the winds, in favor of mass consumerism, increasing personal and government debt, and, for those who couldn't keep up, an addictive welfare state that has resulted in several generations of people living in "council houses," having no expectation of ever working, and taking offense at those who tell them they should find a job. Perhaps it could be called the age of entitlement.

There are always downsides to affluence, regardless of what lottery promoters and prosperity gospel preachers may say. Governments and individuals who ignore warnings like this one do so at their own risk: "Whoever loves money never has enough; whoever loves wealth is never satisfied with their income. This too is meaningless" (Eccl. 5:10).

THE DECLINE

Shortly before World War I, Britain had begun to fade from its position as "workshop of the world." Its economy stopped growing as fast as it had in the past, and inevitably the nation began a slow but steady decline, relative to other countries.

There are many theories about why this happened, including less demand for British products overseas. A significant contributing factor was complacency, the notion that things will always remain the same, which predictably leads to laziness, lack of productivity and incentive, and inevitably decline. Consider one of many passages in Scripture that warns of the consequences of laziness: "Lazy hands make for poverty, but diligent hands bring wealth" (Prov. 10:4).

Is there a lesson here for us? I believe there is, and to understand it, we must fast-forward to the mid-twentieth century.

On April 20, 1968, Enoch Powell, a member of the British

House of Commons, delivered a speech to a Conservative Association meeting in Birmingham, England. It was dubbed the "Rivers of Blood" address, and Powell was denounced as a racist by liberal elites for his mentioning of "the black man" overtaking "the white man" because of immigration.

Whatever the legitimacy—or illegitimacy—of such a charge, Powell's larger point was this: no nation can maintain its character if it doesn't control its borders and limit immigration to an orderly pace so as to make sure those entering the country can be assimilated and fully embrace the values, language, and culture of the host nation.

Look at it this way. If I have a glass of water and begin pouring milk into it, the milk will first dilute and then eventually replace the water in the glass. It is the same with immigration. No nation can survive in its current form if it fails to control who enters it, how many enter it, and what will be done to make sure that the immigrants are fully assimilated and have the skills necessary to find jobs, so they can be contributors to the nation instead of burdening taxpaying citizens.

There is no right, in law or in logic, for anyone to claim residence in a country in which they do not enjoy citizenship. Whenever I travel to foreign lands, a stamp on my passport not only limits my stay but in many cases informs me that I am not allowed to work in that country. I never complain. It is their right. If I want to stay longer—and especially if I want to work in that country—I must receive permission by way of a visa or other document permitting me to do so.

"Is Europe Committing Suicide?" read a headline in the May 20, 2017, *Daily Mail* newspaper. In a review of Douglas Murray's book *The Strange Death of Europe: Immigration, Identity, Islam*, Dominic Sandbrook wonders if Europe is deliberately contributing to its own decline. The subheading in his review says, "Controversial book claims elites in UK and the

Continent are encouraging mass immigration because they've lost faith in historical Christian values."[12]

Perhaps that is because they haven't applied those values. At any rate, what would make European leaders favor Islamic values, given the deplorable way they are practiced in Muslim-majority nations?

In his book, Murray writes, "By the end of the life spans of most people currently alive, Europe will not be Europe and the peoples of Europe will have lost the only place in the world we had to call home."[13]

Sandbrook continues his review:

The causes, [Murray] thinks, are twofold. First, our political leaders have knowingly colluded in the "mass movement of peoples into Europe," filling "cold and rainy northern towns" with "people dressed for the foothills of Pakistan or the sandstorms of Arabia."

Second, he believes Europe's intellectual and cultural elites, including those in Britain, have "lost faith in its beliefs, traditions and legitimacy." Crippled with guilt, obsessed with atoning for the sins of empire, they have lost sight of the historic Christian values that their people expect them to defend.

As a result of their deluded utopianism, Murray thinks, Europe is ceasing to be Europe. Indeed, he believes that European culture as generations have understood it—the culture of Michelangelo and Mozart, Shakespeare and Goethe, Dickens and Wagner—is doomed.[14]

It's a depressing outlook, but the reality he describes is one of Britain's and the rest of Europe's own making and could even now be reversed if leaders have the will and stop feeding at the trough of political correctness.

CAMEO: *George Stephenson (1781–1848)*

George Stephenson was the principal inventor of the locomotive. People tend to forget what life was like before all of our modern conveniences. Prior to the invention of machines that allowed people to travel between towns and even countries and then across oceans and continents by air and eventually into space, for thousands of years modes of transportation consisted of walking or riding horses (or elephants).

The invention of the steam engine and locomotive revolutionized land transportation, much as the building of oceangoing ships had done to promote commerce by sea. Railroads not only allowed for the transport of large numbers of goods but also made it possible for people to travel to places they never would have thought to visit by horse and cart, unless they were of the sturdiest stock.

While the railroads supplanted horse-drawn transportation, they opened up many markets, instead of closing them as critics claimed they would. There have always been those opposed to progress, believing the familiarity of the status quo is preferable to a future which no one can predict. Stephenson's bravery and commitment to the future contributed greatly to the expansion of the British Empire and its ability to sustain itself into the twentieth century. His work ethic and vision were once taught in British (and American) schools, before those virtues were replaced by more self-centered concerns.

As if this weren't discouraging enough for Britain and the rest of the English-speaking world, the *Daily Mail* in 2015 published a lengthy investigative report that found "eighty-five Islamic courts dispensing 'justice' across the UK."[15]

There is disagreement over what constitutes an Islamic court. Some are councils without authority over British law and deal mostly with religious matters, including marriage and divorce. But the following case, one of many from the article, is a profile of what these courts or councils dispense, and it isn't justice, especially not for women.

The newspaper reported on a young Muslim woman who sits before a cleric and complains about the state of her marriage. She claims her husband has physically and emotionally abused her and "treats me like a dog." Instead of offering an empathetic response, the *Daily Mail* reports, "the cleric laughs and says, 'Why did you marry such a person?'"[16]

Any nation such as Britain that allows for a people who do not hold Western values to invade it will not remain that country for long. The Muslim invasion of Europe is replacing Western culture with Islamic culture. If the trend continues, there will be nothing left of the West. Radical Muslims announce that this is their plan and ultimate objective. The West remains mostly in denial, refusing to defend itself. Unless things are reversed, the outcome for Britain and Europe is predictable.

But none of this is inevitable. Yes, to the casual observer of what is happening in Great Britain, the situation seems hopeless. But Christians are a people of hope, believers in lost causes for the sake of God's kingdom. At one point in Britain's history, the abolition of slavery appeared to be a lost cause, until a man of faith decided to fight because of his Christian principles. William Wilberforce fought for more than forty years in a battle that turned even his friends against him. You could say he gave his life for this fight, dying just three days after learning that the Slavery Abolition Act had become law.

The problem in Britain and elsewhere is that those holding to the Christian faith are in decline. It is difficult to have influence on culture and government when the overwhelming majority is secular or only nominally Christian and view faith, if they view it at all, as a private matter.

WHAT CAN WE LEARN FROM GREAT BRITAIN?

The United States is currently engaged in a hotly contested—and highly politicized—debate over immigration. As the politicians fight it out, let me offer my perspective and then some practical suggestions for injecting the values of our faith into the equation.

If we have learned anything from the British experience, it is this: every nation has the right and responsibility to control its borders. That means finding ways to ensure those coming into our country do so for the right reasons, as well as setting limits based on our resources and capabilities for receiving immigrants. There is nothing un-Christian about creating and maintaining an orderly process that must be adhered to by anyone seeking entry into our country. Nor is it unfair or prejudicial to refuse entry to anyone for whom there is credible evidence that they may be connected with criminal or terrorist activity. Controlling our borders is just plain common sense, a trait that the Brits seem to have abandoned.

What intrigues me most, however, about Enoch Powell's "Rivers of Blood" speech[17] is what I call the rest of the story: we control our borders "to make sure those entering the country can be assimilated and fully embrace the values, language and culture of the host nation." A friend recently shared a story with me about a stay-at-home mom who volunteered through her church to "adopt" a young Syrian family who had recently (and legally) immigrated to her city. For more than a year, she took the young mom to the grocery store once a week, offered free babysitting so both parents could attend an English language class (offered by her church). She took her to a vacant parking lot and taught her how to drive, just as she once had done for her own teenage kids. Today both parents speak English well enough to get along on their own and are now in the process of applying for citizenship. The dad found a job in IT, further exposing him to Western values.

It's just one person, with no formal training in cross-cultural ministry. Only one small family from a nation many would consider an enemy of the United States. But that's often how serious problems are solved. One at a time.

In the same way that Britain was unable to maintain its dominance over regions with different histories, languages, and religions, the country began to import immigrants, many of whom represented those nations where British influence once dominated. It isn't a stretch to say that what Britain experienced (and what many believe America is now experiencing) is a kind of cultural suicide. When people will not assimilate and embrace the character and values of their host nation, that nation is not likely to sustain itself on the foundation that made it great in the first place.

As citizens of the kingdom of God, you have both a responsibility and a privilege to come alongside the "aliens and strangers" in your communities and demonstrate a way of life and a belief system that will give them a full and abundant life.[18] That will make us all proud to call them neighbors, friends, and fellow citizens—and possibly, through your practical witness to them, fellow believers.

CHAPTER 8

THE RUSSIAN EMPIRE:
From Orthodoxy to Communism

MEN HAVE FORGOTTEN GOD.
—*Alexandr Solzhenitsyn*

Russia may be unique among the empires and superpowers considered in this book. It doesn't precisely follow the pattern suggested by Sir John Glubb, and over the centuries it has manifested itself in different ways, most notably in modern times as the Soviet Union, an empire of its own. The Soviet Union collapsed under the weight of failed socialism, failed Communism—and its accompanying atheism, with attempts to eradicate the Jewish and Christian faiths—and a failed policy of overreach in which it imposed itself by force and deceit on other nations. It was pushed into collapse, one might say, by the fervent opposition of US president Ronald Reagan and his massive defense buildup, which the Soviets could not match, and his coordinated opposition with British prime minister Margaret Thatcher and the fiercely anti-Communist Polish pope John Paul II. Soviet practices did bear some resemblance to that of other empires and great nations that are either no more or exist as mere shadows of their former selves.

CAMEO: *Nicholas II*

If there was ever a case of the wrong man leading a nation at the wrong time, Nicholas II was that man. He was as ready to be a leader of Russia as I am to be an astronaut. Neither his upbringing nor his attitude qualified him for the post. If he had been a worker seeking a job, any employer looking at his resume would have turned him down flat. But as England and other countries have experienced, succession doesn't always bring the best people to the top.

While he received a military education, his preferences were more in line with those of other young Russians of his time. Nicholas loved physical exercise, but when it came to exercising his brain through intellectual pursuits, he was a couch potato.

Nicholas had great personal charm, which modern politicians desire, but surprisingly failed to use that trait to his benefit, shunning contact with his subjects in favor of spending time with his inner circle and family.

In 1894, he married Alexandra, who possessed the strength of character he lacked. Alexandra exercised an unusual amount of power over her husband, seeking the advice of spiritualists and faith healers, on whom he came to increasingly rely. The most famous among them was Rasputin, a self-described holy man, who came to acquire great power over them both.

Under the influence of Rasputin, Nicholas came to believe his authority was confirmed directly upon him by God, to whom he was solely responsible. (Sound familiar?)

As the *Encyclopaedia Britannica* notes, "His dedication to the dogma of autocracy was an inadequate substitute for a constructive policy, which alone could have prolonged the imperial regime."[1]

His refusal to compromise (he was, after all, doing God's bidding) brought on political and eventually social chaos. The Bolsheviks were gaining strength by appealing to the masses about income and political inequality.

On March 8, 1917, riots erupted in Petrograd (now Saint Petersburg). Nicholas ordered troops to restore order, but by then it was too late. The government resigned, and Nicholas was forced to renounce the throne—not in favor of his son, Alexis, but in favor of his brother Michael, who refused the crown.

Not long after that, the Bolsheviks seized power, murdering Nicholas and his family.

Would things have turned out differently had Nicholas II been a better leader? It is difficult to second-guess history, but clearly his incompetence hastened the rise of what became the Soviet Union, which, especially under Joseph Stalin, was responsible for the murder of tens of millions of Russians over its seven-decade existence.

THE AGES OF PIONEERS AND CONQUESTS

The Russian Empire is generally divided into two eras: from the end of the Great Northern War in 1721 and later the Communist Revolution in 1917. From 1650 onward, the medieval duchy of Muscovy, centered in the city of Moscow, grew and changed into what we now consider the country of Russia. Russia has always been a middle ground between Europe and Asia. Russia became Christian long before the Nordic nations did. However, at the same time, from 1250 until 1480, Russia remained a tribute-paying extension of the Mongol Empire. By the time Peter I (later known as Peter the Great) assumed power in 1682 (he was appointed ruler at the tender age of ten by a council of Russian nobles with his mother as regent), Russia had expanded its territory to the Baltic and Black Seas as well as to the Pacific Ocean.

Prior to Peter I (1672–1725), Russia was estranged from Europe and far inferior technically, administratively, and socially. However, Peter's predecessors had managed to expand Russian control eastward to the Pacific. Think of it as the Wild, Wild East—vast but barely explored, other than sparsely populated areas of land.

As in America, this void caused people to migrate to empty spaces, where they settled and tried to build their lives. Thus for many years, there was widespread eastward movement within Russia. However, landlords in the west wished to maintain their labor source, and with the support of the tsar, they established a system of serfdom different from that in the rest of Europe and more aligned with American slavery. Serfs were bound to the land they were born on and could be sold without the land they were supposed to work. They could also be killed at will, and if they tried to escape, they could be arrested and returned to their owner.

Government

If you had to state the purpose of the American government, what would it be? Is it to take care of its citizens? Some people think so. These are folks who believe they are entitled to certain things, mostly the income others have earned and the taxes they have paid. Not always, but it seems increasingly so.

Yes, protecting the American people from enemies and keeping us safe is a primary function of government. And yet does this answer the question about the purpose of government, and if not, where do we look for an adequate and satisfying answer?

One can find the answer in the inspired words of Thomas Jefferson, who wrote the first draft of the Declaration of Independence from Great Britain and then labored over its several revisions in a small flat in Philadelphia.

After writing of how our rights are given to us by our Creator, Jefferson makes this strong point: "And to secure these rights, governments are instituted among Men."

To secure what rights? Why, the rights God has endowed in us.

Why is that necessary?

Because, as James Madison wrote, if men were angels, government would not be necessary. The fact that we are not angels suggests we must be prevented from submitting to our lower nature, which, if left uncontrolled, can lead to anarchy, and anarchy is the opposite of promoting the general welfare.

If we will not be controlled by God, then we must be controlled by the state, acting "under God." That is what Paul says in Romans 13. The distinction is an important one because not all governments are under God. Perhaps none are. Not fully, or even mainly. Sixty million abortions (and counting) and the rest of the list of things God calls abominations seem to me to prove that America is not, and perhaps never has been, "under God." More on that in the final chapter.

Increasingly, the United States seems bent on going its own way, the way other nations have gone. We say "under God" in our Pledge of Allegiance (the phrase was added during the Eisenhower administration, during a period of fierce anti-Communism in response to that godless philosophy), but do we mean it in ways that are observable? Do we practice submission to God and his will, laws, and precepts, instituted for the good of individuals as well as of nations? It is increasingly difficult to discern.

Peter the Great was no fool. He knew of Western superiority, as he had spent a great deal of time in the German quarter of Moscow. He also had briefly lived in Holland and England. Between 1697 and 1698, he traveled through Europe, where he recruited a thousand experts to help modernize Russia. Peter's main foreign enemy was Sweden, which controlled the Baltic States and thus what Russia prized more than almost anything: a warm-water port. A series of military conflicts ensued, culminating in the Great Northern War of 1700–1721. A long list of crushing defeats forced Peter to import officers and technicians for his army to give it a chance of defeating the Swedes, who at the time had the finest army in the world. That seems hard to imagine when one considers modern Sweden.

In 1708, during the Great Northern War, King Charles XII of Sweden invaded Russia, forcing Peter to do what Russia normally does in winter: retreat across the plains and wait for the cold and snow. As Napoleon and Hitler would later learn, you don't mess with a Russian winter. The winter of 1708–1709 dramatically weakened the Swedish army, and they were crushed. Peter would go on to conquer the Baltic States, and once the Treaty of Nystad was signed in 1721, ending the Great Northern War, Russia was officially recognized as having control of the Baltic States. The empire was born.

THE AGE OF COMMERCE, AFFLUENCE, AND INTELLECT

I've combined these ages because Russia doesn't have a significant period of intellect and commerce. When led by competent leaders like Peter and Catherine the Great (1729–1796), the empire modernized and grew in strength. The rest of the time, incompetent tsars squandered numerous opportunities to grow the country. Wars would be fought continually on the edge of the empire, against nearly every bordering nation, over access to the sea and to establish Russian influence over the Slavic peoples of Eastern Europe.

This is not to say the Russian tsars failed to attempt to bring modernization to Russia. Catherine the Great practiced what has been called enlightened despotism. While Europe proper underwent the Age of Enlightenment, Russia absorbed European thought and culture.

No Europeans studied Russian thinkers at this time, but European thinkers were well known in Russia. While under Catherine the Great, the Russian Court conversed in French and read Voltaire, but no real progress was made in reforming serfdom in Russia. Thus a true age of commerce, affluence, and intellect never came to pass. Serfs who were determined to free themselves from conditions disturbingly similar to slavery did attempt to rebel. After all, they had no other way to try to better their lives. However, after the suppression of Pugachev's Rebellion (1773–1775), the already miserable state of serfs in Russia declined further, and the government took measures even more severely oppressive.

Russian serfs were bought and sold by aristocrats, as were slaves in America. Serfs were bound to serve the local lord for life, unless they were sold. So were their children. Movement of serfs was restricted to prevent migration, and careful records were maintained to enforce this and to ensure that in the absence of an obvious mark (like skin color in America), serfs could be identified, so that no serf could improve his station.

The retention of serfdom severely hampered economic growth. Who would have guessed that a feudal system of economics would not work in the modern world? No amount of European culture, no number of visiting thinkers, scientists, or economists could bring about greatness to Russia as long as the serfs remained enslaved. Russia was ultimately a state in which the aristocracy accepted the authority of the monarchy and in exchange received complete authority over the serfs. The Russian state with serfdom was essentially a national slave state on a scale that vastly exceeded the scale of slavery in the American South. Even Russia's defeat of Napoleon (1812), with considerable assistance from the harsh winter conditions, was only a temporary boost to Russian influence and power.

Despite its shortcomings, the Russian Empire produced great works of art and literature. Fine art in Russia dates back to the Stone Age. Google it and be amazed. However, the achievements of the educated upper classes did not reflect growth for the country as a whole. Failure of the government to provide economic reforms, and a growing trend of military defeats, including the disastrous Crimean War and World War I, led to the empire's fall and the rise of the dark shadow of Communism, first in Russia and then as a primary political and economic export to other countries. A century of turmoil and war set up Russia for the Bolshevik Revolution in 1917, which was quickly followed by the imposition of Communism on the nation.

Ultimately, however, Russia was held together by its army, and its expansion was led by the army. It was the army that insured the serfs were held in line, and the serfs provided the slave labor necessary to support the army. The tsars could then use the army to enforce their chosen foreign policy.

THE DECLINE

It was about the Soviet Empire that the great Russian novelist Alexandr Solzhenitsyn spoke in an address he gave on receiving the 1983 Templeton Prize for Progress in Religion. I highly recommend you read the speech in its entirety; it can be found for free online.[2]

His address and a subsequent speech at Harvard could serve as editorials, even prophecies, for our time, if indeed modern editorialists thought about things higher than this earthly kingdom. The most profound sections of his speech stated and repeated a single theme: "If I were called upon to identify briefly the principal trait of the *entire* twentieth century, here too, I would be unable to find anything more precise and pithy than to repeat once again: Men have forgotten God."[3] The elites hated it, as did editorial writers at major newspapers, but Solzhenitsyn demonstrated that he saw, better than most Westerners, where the West was headed. It was Solzhenitsyn who exposed the Soviet gulags and eventually came to lecture the West, which he saw experiencing its own decline. The West treated him as a hero before his warnings. After those speeches, he was ignored, even rejected, by some of the same people who had once hailed his name and courage.

The Russian Empire, in its many incarnations and manifestations, is depressing, not only to those who read about it but even more so to those who had to endure it. During most of the existence of the Russian Empire, there were just two classes. If you were not part of the nobility, you were a serf, a virtual slave to the landowner to whom you were attached. This social and financial gap served as fuel for the Russian Revolution in the early twentieth century.

CAMEO: *Catherine the Great (1729–1796)*

Catherine the Great has always fascinated and delighted historians. Perhaps it is because she was a rare female leader in an era dominated by men.

Make no mistake, though. She was as strong and resolute as any man. She even orchestrated a coup against her husband, who had ascended to the throne barely six months earlier. Catherine expanded Russia's borders and ruled for more than three decades in the late eighteenth century.

Catherine's life was the stuff of the History and Playboy Channels. Her "love life" was more lust than love. In 1745, she married Russia's grand duke Peter, who was regarded as immature and juvenile. He preferred toys and mistresses to Catherine, and she preferred books and reading to him, though she would quickly pile up her own list of lovers.

The website *Biography.com* picks up the story, which reads like a novel.

By the time Peter ascended to the throne, he was openly cruel to his wife and considered pushing her aside to allow his mistress to rule with him. A few days after his resignation, he was strangled while in the care of Catherine's co-conspirators at Ropsha, one of Peter's estates. The exact role the empress played in her husband's death is unclear.

According to most accounts, Catherine had around 12 lovers during her life. She had a system for managing her affairs—often bestowing gifts, honors and titles on those she liked, in order to win their favor. At each relationship's end, Catherine usually found a way to get her new paramour out of her hair. Gregory Potemkin, perhaps her most significant lover, spent many years as her favorite, and remained lifelong friends after their passions cooled.[4]

Like other rulers (see "Nicholas II"), Catherine believed in absolute rule, though she did make some attempts at political and social reforms. Again, *Biography.com* gives details.

> She put together a document, known as the "Nakaz," on how the country's legal system should run, with a push for capital punishment and torture to be outlawed and calling for every man to be declared equal. Catherine had also sought to address the dire situation of country's serfs, workers who were owned by landowners for life. The Senate protested any suggestion of changing the feudal system.
>
> After finalizing the Nakaz, Catherine brought delegates together from different social and economic classes to form the Legislative Commission, which met for the first time in 1767. No laws came out of the commission, but it was the first time that Russians from across the empire had been able to express their thoughts about the country's needs and problems. Ultimately, the Nakaz became more known for its ideas rather than its immediate influence.[5]

Perhaps more than any other Russian leader before or since (not counting the Communist takeover, in the twentieth century, of Eastern Europe, a region that was never part of Russia), Catherine expanded Russia's borders, mostly by military adventures.

In November of 1796, Catherine suffered a stroke, and she died a day later. While many remember her, if they remember her at all, for her numerous affairs, she did achieve some formidable goals, such as reforming education and being a champion of the arts. The serfs, however, remained of little concern, and that festering boil would come back to torment Russia a century later, leading to the Bolshevik Revolution and the imposition of Communism on the country.

Biographies have been written about Catherine the Great, and they are as fascinating as she was.

CHAPTER 9

THE UNITED STATES:
1776–?

SURELY THE NATIONS ARE LIKE A DROP IN
A BUCKET; THEY ARE REGARDED AS DUST
ON THE SCALES; HE WEIGHS THE ISLANDS
AS THOUGH THEY WERE FINE DUST.
—*Isaiah 40:15*

GOD BLESS AMERICA.
—*Irving Berlin (and most presidents)*

Whenever I hear the song "God Bless America" sung at baseball games and patriotic events, I ask myself, *Why should he?*

Like ancient Israel—the only nation ever to enjoy a covenant relationship with God—which was exiled because of its unfaithfulness to God and his requirements, America doesn't seem to be doing much that would find favor in God's sight.

A lot of people have made a lot of money by claiming that the United States has a special, even unique, relationship with God. Their evidence ranges from economic prosperity, to military might, to the large number of churches spread across the country, to statements made by our founders and by subsequent political and even religious leaders about divine providence, backed by quotations from Scripture. It all sounds good, but when I look at the arc of this empire, it appears to me that we've passed through each of Sir John Glubb's stages—pioneers, conquests, commerce, affluence, intellect—and are fully engaged in the age of decadence.

Ignored by those who cite a litany of proofs of God's blessing of America are the sixty million abortions (as of 2019); the mainstreaming of what used to be considered aberrant and abhorrent relationships, now openly displayed; various other corruptions of maleness and femaleness to the extent that in Oregon and Washington, DC (and probably more places soon), we have "gender neutral" designations on driver's licenses; serial murders in major cities; cohabitation; marital breakdown; ethical violations in business and government; a coarseness and corrosion of culture that includes but is not limited to the multibillion-dollar pornography industry; and the abandonment of a standard by which we once distinguished right from wrong. This list is not exhaustive, and it likely labels me old-fashioned, out of touch, or intolerant, which only confirms how far we've fallen from what we once were.

The apostle Paul writes in Romans 1:30, "They invent ways of doing evil." The evils known to us are insufficient to satisfy our insatiable desires, so we invent new ones. How reflective this is of the darkness of the unredeemed soul.

Ancient Israel was destroyed for sins similar to ours. What makes those promoting supposedly righteous America think we can escape judgment—or, if you prefer a nonreligious conclusion, avoid suffering the consequences of our chosen behavior? And it *is* chosen by each of us. We either willingly participate in it or are willingly indifferent to it, allowing the rot to progress, just as ignoring a termite infestation will undermine the foundation of your home.

The major media in Hollywood and New York promote these evils and are coconspirators in our decline, and when they are criticized, they defend themselves by saying they are just giving the people what they want. This is like saying you didn't rob a bank but only drove the getaway car. Under the law, you are just as guilty when you give the robbers what they want, a chance to get away.

In what is known as the church age, we do not find God throwing down judgment on us for violating his laws, decrees, and precepts. But we do find that we suffer the consequences for ignoring him, just as we suffer immediate consequences from ignoring gravity by jumping off a tall building.

The late Roman Catholic bishop Fulton J. Sheen said it best in the mid-twentieth century. Then it was a very different America. He could have been prophesying about today when he observed, "America, it is said, is suffering from intolerance. It is not. It is suffering from tolerance: tolerance of right and wrong, truth and error, virtue and evil, Christ and chaos. Our country is not nearly so much overrun with the bigoted as it is overrun with the broad-minded. The man who can make up his mind in an orderly way, as a man might make up his bed, is called a bigot; but a man who cannot make up his mind, any more than he can make up for lost time, is called tolerant and broad-minded."[1]

I love America. I am privileged—even blessed, if I may use that word—to have been born in this country through no choice of my own. With the possible exception of Ireland, there is no country in which I would rather live my earthly life, but it is not my home. Heaven is my home and destination, and while I want to preserve for my children and their children the freedoms I have enjoyed, the Scriptures foretell a day when everything that currently is will no longer be.

If you stay overnight in a hotel, would you call an interior decorator should the wallpaper not be to your liking? No, because it is not your home. If your house is on fire, would you be thinking of painting it?

CAMEO: *Thomas Jefferson (1743–1826)*

There are many who could qualify as the most influential person in the ascent of the United States, but if I had to pick one, it would have to be Thomas Jefferson. Though a deist who edited his own Bible, cutting out the parts he didn't like, Jefferson understood that in order for our rights to be protected, they must be put out of the reach of government.

Like John Locke, Jefferson helped destroy the "divine right of kings" belief embraced by ancient rulers. Kings used to determine people's rights (which were often limited and changeable at the whim of the king), but Jefferson wrote in the Declaration of Independence that human rights were given to us by our Creator and thus could not—and should not—be tampered with by monarchies or other institutions established by men and women.

That the first right of all—the right to life—was tampered with by the Supreme Court in the infamous 1973 decision known as *Roe v. Wade* does not repeal the truth of Jefferson's words.

The Declaration was the philosophical underpinning upon which the other Founders, most notably James Madison, built the Constitution and thus the nation. Without the Declaration, it might have been impossible for the Constitution to have been written, and likely it and the nation would not have survived for as long as it has. Other nations have written constitutions, but most of them were not established on the type of base on which the US was founded.

On the 150th anniversary of the Declaration of Independence, our thirtieth president, Calvin Coolidge, delivered an address that linked the founding of the nation to religious principles dating back to the great preachers of the eighteenth century. The following paragraph is of particular significance in a rapidly growing secular age.

A spring will cease to flow if its source be dried up; a tree will wither if its roots be destroyed. In its main features the Declaration of

Independence is a great spiritual document. It is a declaration not of material but of spiritual conceptions. Equality, liberty, popular sovereignty, the rights of man—these are not elements which we can see and touch. They are ideals. They have their source and their roots in the religious convictions. They belong to the unseen world. Unless the faith of the American people in these religious convictions is to endure, the principles of our Declaration will perish. We cannot continue to enjoy the result if we neglect and abandon the cause.[2]

Are we neglecting and abandoning the cause behind our founding? Would Jefferson recognize the nation he helped create?

America is headed for foreclosure. We are drowning in financial debt and submerged under an immoral tsunami. At the end of 2018, the US national debt was approaching $22 trillion, and the deficit was at $985 billion. Both are growing. These are unsustainable numbers. If not addressed, they will lead us ultimately into bankruptcy and possibly another depression.

Our politicians are unwilling to do much about the financial debt, because they fear being called names by their opponents who will accuse them of not caring about children or senior citizens. Recall a political ad that responded to the plan of Representative Paul Ryan (a Republican from Wisconsin) to reform Social Security and Medicare. His plan was a serious proposal about a serious problem that needs to be addressed. The ad showed a Ryan look-alike pushing an elderly woman in a wheelchair over a cliff. It was a juvenile attack, but fear works better than solving problems for politicians whose main goal is to get reelected. If a problem were actually solved, what issues would politicians have to run on?

As to our moral decline, the day when citizens heeded cries for repentance have been overcome by the prosperity gospel and high-living TV evangelists. Megachurches are filled with people who don't want to hear sermons about sin but prefer sermons about happiness, pleasure, health, and material wealth.

Dr. Charles Stanley has put it well: "We have moved from the day of Samuel who said, 'Speak, Lord, for thy servant heareth,' to our present day when we say, 'Listen, Lord, for thy servant speaketh.'"[3]

The motto of the Stony Brook School in New York is "Character Before Career." In our modern political and socially dysfunctional era, it is more like career, personal pleasure, and affluence before character—if we ever get to character. Character presumes a standard by which we can judge who has good character and whose character is bad. But that requires we have a definition of good and bad, and to suggest that one exists puts one in danger of a lawsuit from the ACLU, a litigious parent, or an activist student. Such standards were jettisoned in the 1960s, and we continue to pay the price today, wherever the spirit of the age reigns.

Knowing how we got to this point is crucial to finding our way out, though absent a revival, like the one in 1857—which was true divine intervention—it may be too late.

As my fellow columnist Pat Buchanan wrote following the August 2017 violence in Charlottesville, Virginia, between a small group of white supremacists, neo-Nazis, and alt-rightists and a group of hardcore leftists, "What has changed is America herself. She is not the same country. We have passed through a great social, cultural and moral revolution that has left us irretrievably divided on separate shores."[4]

Does history teach us nothing? It teaches us everything, but it seems fewer are paying attention as we embrace the now, and many younger people appear to believe access to the internet is their port of entry to wisdom.

One last thought: why do so many self-declared Christians think God is active only when someone they voted for (mostly Republicans) is elected? Evangelist Franklin Graham said, "God showed up" when Donald Trump was elected president in 2016. So where was God when Barack Obama, Bill Clinton, Jimmy Carter, Lyndon Johnson, and John Kennedy were elected, just to name some modern Democrats? Was he on holiday?

Even evil dictators serve God's purposes, from Nebuchadnezzar to Pontius Pilate to tyrants in modern times, if you believe, as Scripture says, that all authority comes from God.

THE AGE OF PIONEERS

American history—the real history, as opposed to the revisionist variety taught in many public schools and universities—is readily available to any who seek it. The traditional American history I was taught in school began with the "discovery" of America by Christopher Columbus and continued through the Mayflower Compact, the Pilgrims and colonies at Jamestown, the personalities of men like William Bradford, the preaching of Jonathan Edwards and other colonial clergy, and the bravery of George Washington and his troops at Valley Forge, Paul Revere's ride, what the Founders believed and wrote concerning limited government and unlimited personal freedom.

Those who established the new nation believed they had a higher purpose than making money (although that is not a bad motivation). Many believed, rightly or wrongly, they had a divine purpose, and they said so on many occasions. Whether they actually were fulfilling God's will, they thought they were, and that in itself motivated them to stick with it as they confronted and eventually conquered the many challenges ahead.

THE AGE OF INTELLECT

America's earliest universities—Harvard, Yale, Princeton, and Dartmouth—were founded by Christian men who (mostly) lived by biblical principles, and these institutions were established with the goal of educating students by using Scripture as the foundation for their intellectual and spiritual development.

Ever since Harvard College was founded in the seventeenth century, its motto has been *Veritas*, which is Latin for "truth." Unfortunately, at Harvard and so many other universities, truth has become personal and relative, not objective with an immutable source.

Today, in these and other universities across America, God has become an embarrassment, though there are signs of an uptick in interest in the Almighty, chiefly because nothing else seems to be working or satisfying. A class taught at Harvard by professor of psychiatry Dr. Armand Nicholi called "The Question of God: C. S. Lewis and Sigmund Freud Debate God, Love, Sex, and the Meaning of Life" attracted large numbers of students. The quest for life's meaning continues even in a largely secular age.

Speaking at Hillsdale College in 1983, theologian Carl F. H. Henry referenced a remark by the late Harvard president Nathan Pusey, who said "the least that should be expected from a university graduate" is that he or she "pronounce the name of God without embarassment." Dr. Henry added, "That minimum is no longer being met in America today."[5] He continued by noting contrasting approaches to human life and our purpose on earth: one which makes science and intellect supreme and the other which acknowledges the supremacy of God: "Is man but a physically upright and mentally clever animal or does he bear the image, however tarnished, of a holy and merciful personal Creator?"[6]

I'm betting that even the most hardened atheist wishes the story of God's great redemptive plan were true. It is, whether one believes it or not.

Abortion

Since 1973, when the Supreme Court decided to strike down what remained of state laws outlawing or restricting abortion, the battle over the value and meaning of human life has only become more intense.

At bottom, it is about where life comes from, who gives it value, and whether humans are evolutionary accidents or the product of a Creator who endows us with rights and thus places them outside the reach of governments and politicians.

Are we, as the late philosopher-theologian Dr. Francis Schaeffer remarked, "material and energy shaped by pure chance in a random universe" with no author of life, no purpose, and no destination after we die, or are we created in the image and likeness of an objectively existing God who loves us and has a plan for our lives?

These two ideas, or philosophies, are at the heart of the debate over abortion, and so much else.

Scientific advances allow us to see inside the womb with greater clarity than ever before. Babies can be saved at earlier stages of a woman's pregnancy, several weeks earlier than in 1973. No matter. The pro-choice crowd says that unborn life has only the value assigned to it by the woman. If she decides she doesn't want the child, it's a fetus or the product of conception. If she chooses to give birth, it's a child or a baby. The value of the baby doesn't change, having been made in God's image from conception and now able to survive outside the womb at ever earlier stages of development. Pro-abortion groups use euphemisms like "choice" to shift attention from what is being chosen to the woman carrying the child, which is its own form of idolatry because it makes humans the determiner of life's value. Such a philosophy has implications for the other end of life, as well as for physically challenging conditions in between, especially if government has the right to determine who lives and who dies based on its willingness to pay for treatment, something that continues to be debated among politicians. The father of the child he has helped conceive has no rights. If he wants the child and his wife or girlfriend doesn't, she alone gets to make the decision.

If anyone is willing to take the time to see where this can lead, that person should visit Yad Vashem, the memorial to the victims of the Holocaust, in Jerusalem. Some still study the Holocaust (and a few deny it), but it seems we have learned little from it.

For mass killing to be carried out, a regime must devalue lives to the point where their extermination can be accepted by large numbers of people. That is what the Nazis did, and not only to

European Jews but also to gypsies, the handicapped, homosexuals, and others they regarded as barriers to their perfection of the white human race. It is also the avenue that might lead to the devaluing of the elderly and sick as the cost of health care continues to rise and older people are seen as expendable. Don't think this can't happen. That's what people once said about abortion. Euthanasia is a short step away from the abortion clinic, once government gets to decide whose life is valuable and whose is not.

There are ways to fight back against this antilife onslaught, and not just through the political system. Abortion is not the cause of our decadence but a reflection of it. It was G. K. Chesterton who noted that the danger when men stop believing in God is not that they will believe in nothing but that they will believe in anything.

Cole Porter wrote songs for a 1930s show titled called *Anything Goes*. Its title song begins,

In olden days a glimpse of stocking
Was looked on as something shocking,
But now God knows,
Anything goes.

Porter intended it as satire. Today it could be a judgment on modern America.

More than three thousand pregnancy help centers have sprung up across America since *Roe v. Wade* was handed down in 1973. Untold thousands of babies have been saved, and their mothers (and fathers) have been led to faith in Christ and to changed lifestyles and behavior. This has come without any political or judicial involvement.

The volunteers at these centers, and those who have contributed money to their work, have contributed to the decline in the number of abortions in America. These centers offer free services during pregnancy and after the child is born, adoption services, counseling, cash, diapers, and clothes, unlike abortion clinics, which charge for their "services" and who offer no physical or spiritual help. If people want to "make a difference," as the saying goes, they can witness immediate results by volunteering, contributing, or seeking other ways to help these centers tell women the truth and save women from a life of regret, not to mention possible physical harm from abortions gone wrong. The film about Philadelphia abortionist Kermit Gosnell dramatizes the cynicism within the abortion industry. It's titled *Gosnell: The Trial of America's Biggest Serial Killer.*

Courts and legislators will change only when the hearts of Americans change, and that will occur only when people have a different view of life and of God, who created us to be his.

All arguments about abortion have been answered, including who will care for the woman and her child after birth, and if she doesn't want to keep the child, where she can place him or her in a good adoptive home. Only the will to do the right thing remains, and no law alone can force people to do right.

THE AGE OF AFFLUENCE

The United States is the richest nation in the world and the richest in history. Yet perils lie ahead, as they have when other nations experienced periods of great prosperity.

A metaphor that serves as a lesson about decline is the city of Detroit, Michigan. Once a thriving metropolis, its descent into crime, lawlessness, and poverty reflects the downfall of other American cities that in the past were prosperous but because of bad economic, political, and, yes, wrong moral decisions fell from their affluence into poverty, fueled by high crime, falling real estate values, and what became known as white flight.

Detroit is Michigan's largest city. Settled in 1701, it was the first European settlement above tidewater in North America. Its early economy, like that of many other towns and cities in prerevolution days (and well into the nineteenth century), was based on fur trading posts. By the mid-twentieth century, Detroit had evolved into an industrial powerhouse and the country's fourth-largest city. By the end of the twentieth century, Detroit was well on its way to ruin (though recent signs of a comeback provide hope of a turnaround).

Washington, DC, which has had only Democratic mayors and a majority Democratic city council since the 1960s, when Congress gave residents the right to vote for their local leaders, is another city that has had several corrupt politicians. As in Detroit, Washington's policies appear to have ensured a permanent underclass that Democrats can count on for votes, as long as government handouts keep coming.

While there have been periods of economic growth in Detroit over the past fifty years, politicians did not use the money wisely, and the city missed many opportunities to alter its downward trajectory toward more benefits, higher debt, and the discredited notion that constantly raising taxes would stop the bleeding.

The one flaw in a *Detroit Free Press* analysis of the city's past problems is this line: "Although no one could see it at the time, Detroit's insolvency was guaranteed." It isn't that no one could see insolvency coming; it is that they refused to do so. Their attitude was, "Eat, drink, and be merry, for tomorrow we die" (see Isa. 22:13). And so Detroit has succumbed to financial ruin.

There is a grand lesson here not only for other cities faced with similar problems but also for states and especially the federal government, neither of whom want to deny anyone anything, especially in an election year. The lesson is an obvious one, buried deep in our Puritan ethos: You can't spend more than you take in, as though tomorrow will never come. If you do, your tomorrow might just look a lot like Detroit's.

There have been times of great prosperity in America, including the Gilded Age and the Roaring Twenties. These were followed by sharp economic downturns, notably the Great Depression, because too many people in government and in their personal lives did not follow basic economic rules like not spending what you don't have. Having an appearance of affluence is not the same as being affluent.

The federal government encouraged home buying in the 1980s and 1990s. As *Time* magazine noted in an article about whom to blame for the housing and financial crisis of the 1990s, it was "free-wheeling capitalism [that led to] the Gramm-Leach-Bliley Act, which repealed the Glass-Steagall Act, a cornerstone of Depression-era regulation. [President Bill Clinton] also signed the Commodity Futures Modernization Act, which exempted credit-default swaps from regulation. In 1995 Clinton loosened housing rules by rewriting the Community Reinvestment Act, which put added pressure on banks to lend in low-income neighborhoods." Presidents from both parties like to brag that under their administrations, more people owned their own homes than ever before. That was true, but the larger question was, could they afford them? Many could not. They took out adjustable-rate mortgages, and after a few years of low interest rates and low monthly payments, when the interest rate jumped—along with the monthly payment—people couldn't afford it, and the housing boom turned into a bust, leading the way to the 1990s recession.

You might think history would be the best teacher for not living above your means. It would be if people paid attention to history. But the devil gets new material to work with every twenty years, and people think history can teach them nothing. So too many doom themselves to repeat it.

Cities and states headed by liberal politicians often think they can solve problems by taxing the rich more. But in many cases, imposing higher taxes on the wealthy and successful has caused them to flee those cities and states for more tax-friendly places, such as Florida, Alaska, Nevada, South Dakota, Texas, Washington, Wyoming, New Hampshire, and Tennessee, all of which have no state income tax. Their economies seem to be doing well. It's because state government is allowing their residents to save, invest, or spend more of the money they earn, which produces a psychological boost and fuels business investment.

Growing up, I learned three things from my father, and from the example of successful people I admired and wished to emulate, that improve any life. They are inspiration, followed by motivation, followed by perspiration. Today that has flipped to create a sense of envy, greed, and entitlement. The former mostly produced successful and self-sustaining families. The latter has created a permanent underclass with little hope of escape. One political party seems fine with that because it produces more votes for them. They keep the "serfs" dependent on government by claiming the other party will take away their benefits. How cruel.

C. S. Lewis said that prosperity knits a man to this world. He thinks he's finding his place in the world, while the world is actually finding its place in him. Lewis believed that what he called "contented worldliness" is the great enemy of the church.[7]

The late Roman Catholic writer Joseph Sobran put it another way: "I would rather belong to a church that is five hundred years behind the times and sublimely indifferent to change than I would to a church that is five minutes behind the times, huffing and puffing to catch up."

If the church will not sound a prophetic voice, warning a nation of the erosion of its moral underpinnings, who will?

THE AGE OF DECADENCE

> In the time of those kings, the God of heaven will set up a
> kingdom that will never be destroyed, nor will it be left to
> another people. It will crush all those kingdoms and bring
> them to an end, but it will itself endure forever.
>
> —*Daniel 2:44*

Decadence, like cancer, does not always follow the same pattern. It can manifest itself in several ways while leading to the same destination. Some things we see, others we don't. Some things that we think are the cause of decline are actually the result of it.

A 2017 report from the congressional Joint Economic Committee (JEC) is a reminder that the future of America, should the country survive, is based less on what any president can do and more on economic and social trends over which the president, and politicians collectively, has less control. *Washington Post* columnist Robert J. Samuelson summarized the findings of the JEC in his June 12, 2017, column.

Under the category "Family Life," noted Samuelson, the JEC found that the number of people getting married has dropped again from previous years, but the number of people having babies out of wedlock has increased. In 2015, nearly one-third of all children were being raised in single-parent households, or they had no parents at all. That's up from only 15 percent in 1970. Over the same period, births to single mothers increased from 11 percent of all births to 40 percent. In 1970, there were 76.5 marriages for every 1,000 unmarried women over the age of fifteen. By 2015, the rate had dropped to 32 per 1,000.[8]

Broadly speaking, millennials, especially, have suffered through parental divorces and seen in too many cases conditional love. One can understand why they don't want to go through the pain of something similar, so they live together without bothering to get married. The use of the word partner in our vocabulary has almost eradicated the social stigma once attached to "shacking up," or "living in sin," as preachers used to say.

While many women must work outside the home because of economic necessity, and others choose to work for the sheer pleasure of it, couples who have especially young children face challenges, sometimes serious, caused by the need to place them in daycare centers, which lack the nurturing skills only a mother can provide. It's a difficult and often controversial subject, and many books and articles have been written about it, but in my life and experience, moms who choose to stay home (or, yes, stay-at-home dads) have found a more pleasurable outcome than when both parents work in the early years of their child's development.

Societies tend to decline when they lose a sense of transcendent purpose. According to the JEC, fewer Americans feel loyal to any particular religious faith, with about 20 percent of millennials answering "none" when asked about their religious affiliation. In the early 1970s, noted the JEC, about seven in ten adults belonged to a church or synagogue, and slightly more than half attended services at least once a month. Today only about 55 percent have a formal tie to a church or synagogue, and monthly attendance has dropped to about 40 percent.[9]

"Is the Western order becoming irrelevant?" asks a headline in the June 15, 2017, edition of the *Washington Post*. In a review of two books titled *The Fate of the West* and *The Retreat of Western Liberalism*, Carlos Lozada writes, "Superpowers come and go, but it's rare that one puts in for early retirement."[10]

Most of his review is an attack on the Trump presidency, but that first sentence raises a profound and compelling question. And the answer is that all great nations and empires "retire" because of the choices they make, before they are ever conquered by outside forces. If they had remained economically, politically, and especially morally strong, they might have endured, at least beyond their expiration date.

Here's another item from the same newspaper, same month. In a story headlined "A Gap Defined by Values," reporters Jose A. DelReal and Scott Clement write, "The political divide between rural and urban America is more cultural than it is economic, rooted in rural residents' deep misgivings about the nation's rapidly changing demographics, their sense that Christianity is under siege and their perception that the federal government caters most to the needs of people in big cities."[11]

Of course. That's where the big media headquarters are located and where most of the electoral votes are as well.

The story reports on a *Washington Post*–Kaiser Family Foundation survey of nearly 1,700 Americans—including more than 1,000 adults living in rural areas and small towns. It found "deep-seated kinship in rural America, coupled with a stark sense of estrangement from people who live in urban areas. Nearly 7 in 10 rural residents say their values differ from those of people who live in big cities, including about 4 in 10 who say their values are 'very different.'"[12]

The question this poses—but is not asked in the story—is, whose values have the best record of promoting the general welfare, providing for the common defense, and insuring domestic tranquility? This isn't a game in which all ideas and values have equal merit. In our day, we are told they do (unless they are ideas held by conservatives and/or Christians) and that even when those values conflict, it doesn't matter, because it's all about feelings and not objective truth. We fear giving offense more than we fear the consequences that come from buying into ideas that have a track record of error and failure.

Rod Dreher is the author of *The Benedict Option*,[13] a book that has received serious attention in some quarters. It is inspired by the life of a monk who lived in a monastery during the first millennium. In an interview with the publication *American Conservative*, Dreher explained what he means by the "Benedict Option": "It's my name for an inchoate phenomenon in which Christians adopt a more consciously countercultural stance towards our post-Christian mainstream culture. . . . [The] only way to stand firm against the 'barbarians'—people who live by feeling, driven by the passions, not right reason, and with no sense of restraint or obligation beyond satisfying their momentary demands—of our dominant culture is to form stronger, thicker communities based on a commitment to virtue."[14]

Dreher is calling Christians to protect themselves from the corrosive secular culture by forming communities where they and their families can determine which values they live by as well as provide a witness—he uses the word resistance—to the broader culture. There once was a time when Christian values and belief were at least tolerated if not respected, but that time has passed. If we want to retain our faith—and if our country is to survive its expiration date—we must take decisive action to remove ourselves from the mainstream. Have you noticed that the mainstream is often where one finds pollution?

In an op-ed column for the August 2, 2017, edition of the *New York Times*, Dreher calls us to undertake "a brutally honest assessment of both the modern church and the contemporary world. This is painful, but denial will only make the inevitable reckoning worse."[15]

In his own assessment, he points to a 2014 Pew study documenting the falling away from church by Americans, especially millennials, as well as the regression from authentic Christianity to what Notre Dame University sociologist Chris Smith calls a "Moralistic Therapeutic Deism."[16] Moralistic Therapeutic Deism (MTD) is a pseudo-religion that jettisons the doctrines of historical biblical Christianity and replaces them with feel-good, vaguely spiritual nostrums. In MTD, the highest goal of the religious life is being happy and feeling good about oneself. It's the perfect religion for a self-centered, consumerist culture. But it is not authentic Christian faith.[17]

Dreher also calls into question the dubious false and thus unrewarded faith and hope conservative Christians have placed in Republican politics (a subject the late Dr. Edward Dobson and I addressed in our 1999 book *Blinded by Might: Why the Religious Right Can't Save America*). While some gains important to Christians have been made through the efforts of some Republican legislators, this has not stopped the spread of secularism and its consequences. That's because politicians cannot transform human nature, which God reserves for himself. Our problems as a nation are less economic and political and more moral and spiritual. As Dreher eloquently observes, "Too many of us are doubling down on the failed strategies that not only have failed to convert Americans but have also done little to halt the assimilation of Christians to secular norms and beliefs. Mr. Trump is not a solution to this cultural crisis, but rather a symptom of it."[18]

This is a pill many American believers will find hard to swallow, because too many have been raised on and taught a version of a gospel that says America is uniquely blessed of God, for reasons that are becoming increasingly difficult to discern. Dreher warns that if we don't take strong measures to insulate ourselves from the rampant secularism of our culture, we simply will not survive, and the falling away of our children and grandchildren from the faith only confirms his concerns. If you accept the prophecies laid out in both the Old and the New Testaments as true, then the reckoning about which Dreher writes is inevitable, absent a dramatic turnaround and a desire by millions of us to follow a different path.

Trying to slow down the collapse of America through the political system is futile (see Rom. 8:20–21). If reformation and restoration is to occur (and that too is debatable), it will not come from the top down, no matter how righteous government officials appear to be (and there are no righteous individuals, no not one, according to Ecclesiastes 7:20 and Romans 3:10). It can come only from a restored community of believers and from the bottom up, which means it must come from you and from me. It won't be easy.

Given the history of other empires and great nations, the decadence that now is tightening its grip on America almost guarantees our demise, or at the very least a radical decline that will leave the country devoid of the liberties we now enjoy but are rapidly exchanging for a license to do whatever we wish.

I've written about this decline in many of my syndicated columns, so let me summarize what I think are forces fighting against our values—values our culture desperately needs, beginning with the family. According to the much-respected Pew research organization, only 46 percent of American children live in a home with two heterosexual parents. Five percent have no parents and are likely living with grandparents. Contrast that with 1960 demographics that showed 73 percent of children living in what we once called an "intact family."

Marriage is tough, and I am sympathetic to those who have experienced divorce and are doing their best to care for their children. At the same time, we get what we ask for. The baby boom generation, America's largest, campaigned for no-fault divorce and viewed cohabitation as a much-preferred option to marrying someone "until death us do part." Subsequent generations show no signs of improving, as they seem infatuated with entitlement, victimhood, envy, and greed. I can't blame them entirely, because their parents, their schools, and savvy marketers have convinced them that they are the center of the universe.

CAMEO: *Hugh Hefner (1926–2017)*

Many could rightly earn the dishonor of contributing to America's decline, especially in the moral and spiritual realm. Selecting just one is difficult. Those who promoted slavery might qualify. So too those who promoted greed in the Gilded Age of the late nineteenth and early twentieth centuries.

One man, however, perhaps more than any other, is credited (more accurately, blamed) for greasing America's "slouching towards Gomorrah," as the late Judge Robert Bork wrote in his book by that title.

That man is Hugh Hefner, founder of *Playboy* magazine and author of *The Playboy Philosophy*.

As I wrote in a radio commentary when Hefner died in 2017, Hefner was a general in what came to be known as the sexual revolution. His legacy, if one can call it that, ruined lives and families and led to the billion-dollar pornography industry that thrives today. Venereal diseases, some of which have no known cure, are also the bitter fruit of Hefner's bogus ideology.

Whatever fantasies he temporarily fulfilled in some men, he led many into a lifestyle that was bad for women and children—and eventually, bad for men. The testimonies of women associated with Hefner are sad. Hefner operated on a kind of fantasy island, and those who journeyed there often crashed into a sea of brokenness and despair. Many women later told interviewers that they felt used and were discarded like spoiled meat.

The media rarely reported on them, perhaps because media people were frequent guests at Hefner's mansion, attended to by available women.

Hefner divorced love from sex. He told men they not only could but should have sexual relations with any woman, even multiple women. No wonder women began to complain they were having trouble finding men who would be committed to them, while dating and especially in marriage.

In a kind of "which came first, the chicken or the egg," would the sexual revolution have occurred without Hefner? That's like asking whether the American Revolution would have happened without George Washington. Probably yes, in each instance, because in the earlier revolution there were pent-up emotions that led to freedom, and in the later one there were pent-up emotions that led to moral and spiritual (and in some cases medical) bondage.

In what might be considered a reluctant acknowledgment that the lifestyle he recommended for others did not produce positive results for himself, Hefner told Alex Witchel of the *New York Times* in 1992, "I've spent so much of my life looking for love in all the wrong places."[19]

What better epitaph could there be for such a man?

The canned laughter of sitcoms hits its peak when the ten-year-old rolls her eyes as Dad is made to look like a complete idiot. *Ozzie and Harriet* may have been overly idyllic, but David and Ricky never mocked or disrespected their parents for laughs. Kids mimic what they see.

It will take more than a new Supreme Court justice and a Republican majority in Congress to save us from the fate of other empires. It will take a revival of the American spirit, and that can come only through changed attitudes toward our institutions and one another.

Throughout most of our history, each new challenge or period brought with it a sense of optimism about the future. Even during the darkness of World War II, we could sing, "There'll be love and laughter and peace ever after, tomorrow, when the world is free" (from the song "White Cliffs of Dover"). Even if things didn't quite pan out that way, members of the greatest generation moved ahead with hope and optimism. Today that's gone, replaced with a growing sense of foreboding that not only are things pretty bad, but they won't be getting better anytime soon. According to a midsummer Real Clear aggregate of polls, 37.6 percent of those polled believe the country is on the right track, while 56.8 percent say it's on the wrong track.[20] Polls also show that a majority believe the economy is doing well and give President Trump credit. Instead of seeking real solutions, which neither begin nor end in Washington, we just keep stumbling forward, like a man who is lost but refuses to ask for directions.

Clearly, politics can't save us. The rhetoric from both parties has reached a new low. Little if anything is being accomplished to reverse the decadent trends of our times. But is that the role of government, or is moral improvement—the goal of a long-forgotten predecessor to more recent majorities and coalitions—the primary role of believers and of ministers preaching uncompromising biblical messages? Whereas we once could entertain reasonable expectations that our leaders possessed good character regardless of party, our last presidential election (2016) offered a choice between a boastful, superficial, narcissistic misogynist and a corrupt, entitled, shady, lying, unaccomplished politician who ignored her husband's affairs in the pursuit of power. At least that was how these two candidates were presented to voters by partisans.

Another character quality that is in decline is modesty. A Calvin Klein ad features an "upskirt" photo of a young woman's underwear. Victoria's Secret catalogs and shopping mall displays, visible to children, feature barely clad women with come-hither stares. Some of the sexiest films ever made were produced during Hollywood's golden age, when women and men kept on most of their clothes. Films and TV today go for the blatant, mainstreaming sex scenes, flaunting nudity, so much so that a movie's R rating could just as easily stand for "raunchy" as for "restricted." Scriptwriters put words in the mouths of actresses that would make a sailor blush, as the old saying goes. Yet we are supposed to regard this as progress and a demonstration of equality between the sexes.

Do I sound old-fashioned? There is something to be said about old things. Some things endure because they have proved to work for individuals and for society at large. Nations built to last generally sustain traditions and embrace values that brought them success and prosperity. Nations allowed to rot from within with no constraints do just the opposite.

Can America's decline be stopped? Possibly, though the hour is growing late. But any revival of the American spirit won't come through politics and politicians. These have contributed to the problem by not pointing to a better way, informed by history and especially by Scripture. America's central problems are not economic and political; they are moral and spiritual. If not addressed on that level, our doom is sure. If addressed on that level and a genuine spiritual revival occurs, we could be the first nation to prove itself an exception to Sir John Glubb's recording of three thousand years of human history.

One final warning from a conversation the prophet Jeremiah had with God. While it concerned ancient Israel under a different covenant, it still contains a similar warning for our own "wicked and adulterous generation": "If at any time I announce that a nation or kingdom is to be uprooted, torn down and destroyed, and if that nation I warned repents of its evil, then I will relent and not inflict on it the disaster I had planned. And if at another time I announce that a nation or kingdom is to be built up and planted, and if it does evil in my sight and does not obey me, then I will reconsider the good I had intended to do for it" (Jer. 18:7–10).

THERE'S STILL TIME

In light of how far we've regressed, it would be easy to become cynical and give up any hope of rescuing our nation and retreat out of fear and frustration. As people of faith, we are called to be salt and light. Ironically, that is the same terminology used to describe our Lord, which to me means that the only hope for our nation is for individuals like you and me to become Jesus to a culture that has lost its way—to live up to the high moral and ethical standards of the Bible and to demonstrate God's love for the world by reflecting that love in the way we live.

It won't be easy, because it will demand at the very least these things from us:

- Set standards of decency and morality for yourself and your family, including the entertainment you support and the celebrities you elevate (and emulate).

- Gently but firmly guide your children to make wise choices, and provide appropriate discipline when they don't. You are their parents, not their friends.
- Remove your children from government schools and either homeschool them or send them to good Christian schools. Do not send them to universities that have largely become propaganda centers for secular progressives.
- Persevere should your marriage seem not as glamorous as at the beginning, because many will likely be hit with the temptation that constant pleasure and personal satisfaction must always define a good marriage; remember your vows and keep them.
- Temper your skepticism with hope, never allowing it to fall into cynicism and always finding opportunities to lift up what is right and good and true.
- Gather regularly with other believers to worship, to celebrate, and to encourage each other.
- Learn from your failures—whether in marriage, in family, or in work—so as not to repeat them.
- Do whatever you can through adoption, friendships, support of local pregnancy help centers, encouragement, and engagement in the political process to make abortion an unappealing and unnecessary option for women who experience an unplanned pregnancy.
- Daily obey the call to "go and make disciples" (Matt. 28:19), often witnessing without words to show others that a free and abundant life is possible only through faith in Jesus.
- Resist the powerful pull of materialism that draws us into a downward spiral of envy and covetousness, encouraging us to be like everyone else rather than the chosen people of God.

- Understand the role of politics in our free, democratic society by studying candidates and voting according to your convictions and especially biblical truth.
- Contend for your rights as a person of faith, but always respectfully and humbly, even as our Savior faced his Roman captors.
- "Be wise as serpents and innocent as doves" (Matt. 10:16 ESV) when faced with the real and alarming challenge presented by radical Islam.

This list is not exhaustive, and you may have some thoughts of your own to add to it, but you get the idea. We are neither helpless nor hopeless. We have been given all we need through our faith to not just survive but thrive. If you are a liberal Christian, you will likely vote a certain way, and if you are a conservative Christian, you will likely vote the opposite. If that's all you do (and by all means, you absolutely should exercise this right), we will probably sputter along toward that expiration date until this great nation is no different from the ones we've studied here.

As I mentioned at the outset, there are approximately 185 million of us. We will likely differ in our politics, but when it comes to living out the teachings of our King, we have the opportunity to change the wrong direction in which our nation is heading. Christian values have not been lost. They have been abandoned because of neglect and hostility. We have tried to be like everyone else, and we have succeeded. But there is still time.

One hears this verse quoted often, but without discernible results. It is because there does not seem to be genuine repentance in the land and a continuing reliance on especially Republican presidents to deliver us from our collective sins. God spoke these important words to King Solomon: "If my people, who are called by my name, will humble themselves and pray and seek my face and turn from their wicked ways, then I will hear

from heaven, and I will forgive their sin and will heal their land"
(2 Chron. 7:14).

The question is, Who are God's people today? Is it Americans, and if so, what are we doing that God finds favorable?

This verse has been overused in modern times, but its principle is as valid now as when it was spoken. It is not a formula to get what we want—such as personal peace and affluence—but a path toward redemption that begins with the individual and causes ripples that can reach into the highest levels of government. National character is defined not by government but by the placement of a people's hearts and faith.

America may be nearing the end of its road. It has approached the end before. Spiritual revivals, not politicians, rescued us then from the abyss. As J. Edwin Orr has written in his book about the history of revivals in America, all of them came as a result of "a concert of prayer." The social impact of revivals in the United States, as well as in England, was astounding. Crime, drunkenness, and many other social evils were addressed in ways no politician could. When hearts are changed, attitudes are changed, and the result is a changed nation. It never works from the top down but always from the bottom up—or more precisely, from the inside out.

What appears that we like to do the least—pray—is what is most effective in achieving the ends we seek.

It really is up to us, but mostly up to God, who just might respond again with a revival if our intention is to honor him rather than seek pleasure, wealth, and comfort for ourselves. Again, it all begins with a concert of prayer. Are you an instrument in that concert or a disinterested and only part-time spectator?

Ultimately, though, Jesus said, "My kingdom is not of this world" (John 18:36). Keep that at the forefront of your mind as you consider into which kingdom you intend to invest most of your thoughts, time, money, and efforts.

BONUS CAMEOS

There is much to be learned from leaders of empires other than those addressed in this book. Here are two additional cameos on leaders from the European Union.

CAMEO: *Jean Monnet (1888–1979)*

Jean Monnet was a visionary. To my mind, his vision was impaired.

Monnet was a French diplomat and political economist who dreamed of a united Europe similar to the United States. He famously said, "We are not forming coalitions of states, we are uniting men."[1]

The problem was—and is—that unlike in the United States, those European men are parts of states and cultures that have been in conflict with one another for centuries.

Monnet's experience as deputy secretary general of the failed League of Nations from 1919 until 1923 should have disabused him of the notion of trying to unite such disparate factions. The idea that peoples and nations with differing religions, cultures, and histories could be brought together on the basis of nothing better than a dream was folly. The year 2018 may have started the unraveling of the EU, with the beginning of Britain's exit. Others may follow.

Monnet hated war and was passionate about peace (who loves war and hates peace?). He viewed nation-states as obstacles to peace because they always act in their own interests and lust after land and the resources of other states.

As we have seen elsewhere, Monnet ignored the real problem, which is not nation-states but the state of human nature. Only God can alter human nature, or at least redirect it through conversion. The history of man's failed attempts to usher in "peace on earth, goodwill to men" is littered with failure. Even if Monnet rejected a religious solution to the problem of war, history might have taught him the same thing.

Monnet's road to peace was paved with good intentions—to unite the European continent—but we know where that road leads, don't we?

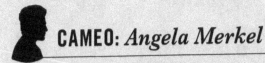

CAMEO: *Angela Merkel*

If Jean Monnet was the father of the European Union, German chancellor Angela Merkel might be said to have contributed to what could be its execution.

Merkel opened Germany's borders to a flood of migrants, mostly from North Africa, who had nothing in common with German culture, religion, or language. Even after growing incidents of violent crime, including rape, Merkel refused to cease what she believed to be a humanitarian effort. Leaders are supposed to look after their own citizens first, but Merkel seemed to want to put Germans last. Perhaps she was pursuing some humanitarian award, like the Nobel Peace Prize.

The unbridled flow of migrants became so bad that the government was unable to account for the whereabouts of one million of them. The country's "easy system" recorded only an asylum applicant's name and country of origin and not much else.

The widely read publication *Der Spiegel* editorialized, "The state stands disgraced and trust is vanishing—and not just when it comes to deportations, but when it comes to everything that a state actually stands for: internal security."[2]

It was the vanished trust in Merkel that caused her to announce in the fall of 2018 she would not seek reelection to another term. Unfortunately, the damage she has caused may be beyond repair.

A PROPHET IGNORED

Why Alexandr Solzhenitsyn, a Russian who had little contact with the United States? The answer is that Solzhenitsyn was a modern-day prophet, telling the West and especially Americans what they did not want to hear but needed to hear. He stood in the line of Old Testament prophets like Jeremiah and Isaiah, who were God's spokesmen. While Scripture teaches that these ancient prophets disappeared with the coming of Jesus of Nazareth, Solzhenitsyn is their worthy successor in the sense that he has spoken truth to the powerful and influential.

In the following two speeches, Solzhenitsyn appeals to America's roots and the values and faith that built the nation and made it unique in history among those that have gained great power and status. He also issues warnings, as I have in this book, that there is a dark and dangerous side to nations that forget their purpose and whom they serve.

First his Templeton Prize address, and then his Harvard speech. Do more than read them. Apply his thoughts to yourself, your community, your state, and ultimately our nation.

The same kind of defect, the flaw of a consciousness lacking all divine dimension, was manifested after World War II when the West yielded to the satanic temptation of the "nuclear umbrella." It was equivalent to saying: Let's cast off worries, let's free the younger generation from their duties and obligations, let's make no effort to defend ourselves, to say nothing of defending others—let's stop our ears to the groans emanating from the East, and let us live instead in the pursuit of happiness. If danger should threaten us, we shall be protected by the nuclear bomb; if not, then let the world burn in Hell for all we care. The pitifully helpless state to which the contemporary West has sunk is in large measure because of this fatal error: the belief that the defense of peace depends not on stout hearts and steadfast men, but solely on the nuclear bomb.

Today's world has reached a stage which, if it had been described to preceding centuries, would have called forth the cry: "This is the Apocalypse!" Yet we have grown used to this kind of world; we even feel at home in it. Dostoevsky warned that "great events could come upon us and catch us intellectually unprepared." This is precisely what has happened. And he predicted that "the world will be saved only after it has been possessed by the demon of evil."

Whether it really will be saved we shall have to wait and see: this will depend on our conscience, on our spiritual lucidity, on our individual and combined efforts in the face of catastrophic circumstances. But it has already come to pass that the demon of evil, like a whirlwind, triumphantly circles all five continents of the earth. . . .

In its past, Russia did know a time when the social ideal was not fame, or riches, or material success, but a pious way of life. Russia was then steeped in an Orthodox Christianity, which remained true to the Church of the first centuries. The Orthodoxy of that time knew how to safeguard its people under the yoke of a foreign occupation that lasted more than two centuries, while at the same time fending off iniquitous blows from the swords of Western crusaders. During those centuries the Orthodox faith in our country became part of the very pattern of thought and the personality of our people, the forms of daily life, the work calendar, the priorities in every undertaking, the organization of the week and of the year. Faith was the shaping and unifying force of the nation.

But in the 17th Century Russian Orthodoxy was gravely weakened by an internal schism. In the 18th, the country was shaken by Peter's forcibly imposed transformations, which favored the economy, the state, and the military at the expense of the religious spirit and national life. And along with this lopsided Petrine enlightenment, Russia felt the first whiff of secularism; its subtle poisons permeated the educated classes in the course of the 19th Century and opened the path to Marxism. By the time of the Revolution, faith had virtually disappeared in Russian educated circles; and amongst the uneducated, its health was threatened.

It was Dostoevsky, once again, who drew from the French Revolution and its seeming hatred of the Church the lesson that "revolution must necessarily begin with atheism." That is absolutely true. But the world had never before known a godlessness as organized, militarized, and tenaciously malevolent as that practiced by Marxism. Within the philo-sophical system of Marx and Lenin, and at the heart of their psychology, hatred of God is the principal driving force, more fundamental than all their political and economic preten-sions. *Militant atheism is not merely incidental or marginal to Communist policy; it is not a side effect, but the central pivot.*

The 1920's in the USSR witnessed an uninterrupted procession of victims and martyrs amongst the Orthodox clergy. Two metropolitans were shot, one of whom, Venia-min of Petrograd, had been elected by the popular vote of his diocese. Patriarch Tikhon himself passed through the hands of the Cheka-GPU and then died under suspicious circumstances. Scores of archbishops and bishops perished. Tens of thousands of priests, monks, and nuns, pressured by the Chekists to renounce the Word of God, were tortured, shot in cellars, sent to camps, exiled to the desolate tundra of the far North, or turned out into the streets in their old age without food or shelter. All these Christian martyrs went unswervingly to their deaths for the faith; instances of apostasy were few and far between. For tens of millions of laymen access to the Church was blocked, and they were forbidden to bring up their children in the Faith: religious parents were wrenched from their children and thrown into prison, while the children were turned from the faith by threats and lies. . . .

For a short period of time, when he needed to gather strength for the struggle against Hitler, Stalin cynically adopted a friendly posture toward the Church. This deceptive game, continued in later years by Brezhnev with the help of showcase publications and other window dressing, has unfortunately tended to be taken at its face value in the West. Yet the tenacity with which hatred of religion is rooted in Communism may be judged by the example of their most liberal leader, Krushchev: for though he undertook a number of significant steps to extend freedom, Krushchev simultaneously rekindled the frenzied Leninist obsession with destroying religion.

But there is something they did not expect: that in a land where churches have been leveled, where a triumphant atheism has rampaged uncontrolled for two-thirds of a century, where the clergy is utterly humiliated and deprived of all independence, where what remains of the Church as an institution is tolerated only for the sake of propaganda directed at the West, where even today people are sent to the labor camps for their faith, and where, within the camps themselves, those who gather to pray at Easter are clapped in punishment cells—they could not suppose that beneath this Communist steamroller the Christian tradition would survive in Russia. It is true that millions of our countrymen have been corrupted and spiritually devastated by an officially imposed atheism, yet there remain many millions of believers: it is only external pressures that keep them from speaking out, but, as is always the case in times of persecution and suffering, the awareness of God in my country has attained great acuteness and profundity.

It is here that we see the dawn of hope: for no matter how formidably Communism bristles with tanks and rockets, no matter what successes it attains in seizing the planet, it is doomed never to vanquish Christianity.

The West has yet to experience a Communist invasion; religion here remains free. But the West's own historical evolution has been such that today it too is experiencing a drying up of religious consciousness. It too has witnessed racking schisms, bloody religious wars, and rancor, to say nothing of the tide of secularism that, from the late Middle Ages onward, has progressively inundated the West. This gradual sapping of strength from within is a threat to faith that is perhaps even more dangerous than any attempt to assault religion violently from without.

Imperceptibly, through decades of gradual erosion, the meaning of life in the West has ceased to be seen as anything more lofty than the "pursuit of happiness," a goal that has even been solemnly guaranteed by constitutions. The concepts of good and evil have been ridiculed for several centuries; banished from common use, they have been replaced by political or class considerations of short-lived value. It has become embarrassing to state that evil makes its home in the individual human heart before it enters a political system. Yet it is not considered shameful to make daily concessions to an integral evil. Judging by the continuing landslide of concessions made before the eyes of our very own generation, the West is ineluctably slipping toward the abyss. Western societies are losing more and more of their religious essence as they thoughtlessly yield up their younger generation to atheism.

If a blasphemous film about Jesus is shown throughout the United States, reputedly one of the most religious countries in the world, or a major newspaper publishes a shameless caricature of the Virgin Mary, what further evidence of godlessness does one need? When external rights are completely unrestricted, why should one make an inner effort to restrain oneself from ignoble acts?

Or why should one refrain from burning hatred, whatever its basis—race, class, or ideology? Such hatred is in fact corroding many hearts today. Atheist teachers in the West are bringing up a younger generation in a spirit of hatred of their own society. Amid all the vituperation we forget that the defects of capitalism represent the basic flaws of human nature, allowed unlimited freedom together with the various human rights; we forget that under Communism (and Communism is breathing down the neck of all moderate forms of socialism, which are unstable) the identical flaws run riot in any person with the least degree of authority; while everyone else under that system does indeed attain "equality"—the equality of destitute slaves. This eager fanning of the flames of hatred is becoming the mark of today's free world. Indeed, the broader the personal freedoms are, the higher the level of prosperity or even of abundance—the more vehement, paradoxically, does this blind hatred become. The contemporary developed West thus demonstrates by its own example that human salvation can be found neither in the profusion of material goods nor in merely making money.

This deliberately nurtured hatred then spreads to all that is alive, to life itself, to the world with its colors, sounds, and shapes, to the human body. The embittered art of the twentieth century is perishing as a result of this ugly hate, for art is fruitless without love. In the East art has collapsed because it has been knocked down and trampled upon, but in the West the fall has been voluntary, a decline into a contrived and pretentious quest where the artist, instead of attempting to reveal the divine plan, tries to put himself in the place of God.

Here again we witness the single outcome of a worldwide process, with East and West yielding the same results, and once again for the same reason: Men have forgotten God.

With such global events looming over us like mountains, nay, like entire mountain ranges, it may seem incongruous and inappropriate to recall that the primary key to our being or non-being resides in each individual human heart, in the heart's preference for specific good or evil. Yet this remains true even today, and it is, in fact, the most reliable key we have. The social theories that promised so much have demonstrated their bankruptcy, leaving us at a dead end. The free people of the West could reasonably have been expected to realize that they are beset by numerous freely nurtured falsehoods, and not to allow lies to be foisted upon them so easily. All attempts to find a way out of the plight of today's world are fruitless unless we redirect our consciousness, in repentance, to the Creator of all: without this, no exit will be illumined, and we shall seek it in vain.

The resources we have set aside for ourselves are too impoverished for the task. We must first recognize the horror perpetrated not by some outside force, not by class or national enemies, but within each of us individually, and within every society. This is especially true of a free and highly developed society, for here in particular we have surely brought everything upon ourselves, of our own free will. We ourselves, in our daily unthinking selfishness, are pulling tight that noose. . . .

Our life consists not in the pursuit of material success but in the quest for worthy spiritual growth. Our entire earthly existence is but a transitional stage in the movement toward something higher, and we must not stumble and fall, nor must we linger fruitlessly on one rung of the ladder.

Material laws alone do not explain our life or give it direction. The laws of physics and physiology will never reveal the indisputable manner in which the Creator constantly, day in and day out, participates in the life of each of us, unfailingly granting us the energy of existence; when this assistance leaves us, we die. And in the life of our entire planet, the Divine Spirit surely moves with no less force: this we must grasp in our dark and terrible hour.

To the ill-considered hopes of the last two centuries, which have reduced us to insignificance and brought us to the brink of nuclear and non-nuclear death, we can propose only a determined quest for the warm hand of God, which we have so rashly and self-confidently spurned. Only in this way can our eyes be opened to the errors of this unfortunate twentieth century and our hands be directed to setting them right. There is nothing else to cling to in the landslide: the combined vision of all the thinkers of the Enlightenment amounts to nothing.

Our five continents are caught in a whirlwind. But it is during trials such as these that the highest gifts of the human spirit are manifested. If we perish and lose this world, the fault will be ours alone.[1]

THE PROPHET'S SECOND WARNING

On June 8, 1978, Alexandr Solzhenitsyn delivered the commencement address at Harvard University. The liberal institution invited him as a hero, but after the speech he was reviled by the Left for his indictment of Western society.

Among the observations Solzhenitsyn made to the graduating class was this:

> A decline in courage may be the most striking feature which an outside observer notices in the West in our days. The Western world has lost its civil courage, both as a whole and separately, in each country, each government, each political party, and, of course, in the United Nations. Such a decline in courage is particularly noticeable among the ruling groups and the intellectual elite, causing an impression of loss of courage by the entire society. Of course, there are many courageous individuals, but they have no determining influence on public life. . . . Should one point out that from ancient times declining courage has been considered the beginning of the end?[1]

Who can credibly present evidence that contradicts Solzhenitsyn's statement?

In the 1970s, a popular book by Robert Ringer was titled

Looking Out for #1. It made the *New York Times* Bestseller List. The book represented the spirit of the age, in which self-interest eclipsed any notion of family, community, or nation.

Returning to Solzhenitsyn: the great author noted, subtly at first and then more directly, the danger when societies rely only on laws made by men and women and do not regard higher laws as preeminent.

> I have spent all my life under a Communist regime and I will tell you that a society without any objective legal scale is a terrible one indeed. But a society with no other scale than the legal one is not quite worthy of man either. A society which is based on the letter of the law and never reaches any higher is taking very scarce advantage of the high level of human possibilities. The letter of the law is too cold and formal to have a beneficial influence on society. Whenever the tissue of life is woven of legalistic relations, there is an atmosphere of moral mediocrity, paralyzing man's noblest impulses. And it will be simply impossible to stand through the trials of this threatening century with only the support of a legalistic structure.[2]

Solzhenitsyn then handed down an indictment that should resonate today, even more than it did at Harvard. "It is feasible and easy everywhere to undermine administrative power and in fact it has been drastically weakened in all Western countries. The defense of individual rights has reached such extremes as to make society as a whole defenseless against certain individuals. . . . It is time, in the West, to defend not so much human rights as human obligations."[3]

Who speaks of obligations today? We even have an all-volunteer military. No one has to inconvenience oneself. Let others pay the price for defending freedom. The rest of us will simply engage in a type of shoplifting, enjoying something for which we have not paid.

And Solzhenitsyn drove his point home in a way that probably made students and administrators squirm, for many of them had been coconspirators in the nation's decline. "Destructive and irresponsible freedom has been granted boundless space. Society appears to have little defense against the abyss of human decadence, such as, for example, misuse of liberty for moral violence against young people, such as motion pictures full of pornography, crime, and horror. It is considered to be part of freedom and theoretically counterbalanced by the young people's right not to look or not to accept. Life organized legalistically has thus shown its inability to defend itself against the corrosion of evil."[4]

Who can define evil in our day? We tolerate everything, even the abortion of sixty million babies (and counting), even the promotion of what used to be called aberrant sexual behavior. The latest is "gender fluidity," which tells people they can decide for themselves what gender they want to be, never mind biology. There are parents who are fine with this, and a government that cares less and less about it.

In our day, the only thing considered evil are persons who stand against what was once considered evil. The moral underpinnings of the nation have shifted like sand at the seashore, and no one seems able—much less willing—to restore them, even if they knew how.

Long before Donald Trump labeled the major media fake news, or before the internet and conservative talk radio came along, Solzhenitsyn delivered his own indictment. Keep in mind this was 1978.

There is no true moral responsibility for deformation or disproportion. What sort of responsibility does a journalist or a newspaper have to his readers, or to his history—or to history? If they have misled public opinion or the government by inaccurate information or wrong conclusions, do we know of any cases of public recognition and rectification of such mistakes by the same journalist or the same newspaper? It hardly ever happens because it would damage sales. A nation may be the victim of such a mistake, but the journalist usually always gets away with it. . . . One may safely assume that he will start writing the opposite with renewed self-assurance.

Because instant and credible information has to be given, it becomes necessary to resort to guesswork, rumors, and suppositions to fill in the voids . . . and none of them will ever be rectified; they will stay on in the readers' memories. How many hasty, immature, superficial, and misleading judgments are expressed every day, confusing readers, without any verification. . . . The press can both simulate public opinion and miseducate it. Thus, we may see terrorists described as heroes, or secret matters pertaining to one's nation's defense publicly revealed, or we may witness shameless intrusion on the privacy of well-known people under the slogan: "Everyone is entitled to know everything." But this is a false slogan, characteristic of a false era. People also have the right not to know and it's a much more valuable one. The right not to have their divine souls [stuffed with gossip, nonsense, vain talk]. A person who works and leads a meaningful life does not need this excessive burdening flow of information.[5]

Solzhenitsyn reached his conclusion by saying America in its decline was not a good role model for what was then the Soviet Union, despite the many indictments he had made in his writings against Communism. And he diagnosed our decline as a failure to uphold a moral, even a religious, sense.

However, in early democracies, as in the American democracy at the time of its birth, all individual human rights were granted because man is God's creature. That is, freedom was given to the individual conditionally, in the assumption of his constant religious responsibility. Such was the heritage of the preceding thousand years. Two hundred or even fifty years ago, it would have seemed quite impossible, in America, that an individual could be granted boundless freedom simply for the satisfaction of his instincts or whims. Subsequently, however, all such limitations were discarded everywhere in the West; a total liberation occurred from the moral heritage of Christian centuries with their great reserves of mercy and sacrifice. . . . State systems were becoming increasingly and totally materialistic. The West ended up by truly enforcing human rights, sometimes even excessively, but man's sense of responsibility to God and society grew dimmer and dimmer. In the past decades, the legalistically selfish aspect of Western approach and thinking has reached its final dimension and the world wound up in a harsh spiritual crisis and a political impasse. All the glorified technological achievements of Progress, including the conquest of outer space, do not redeem the 20th century's moral poverty which no one could imagine even as late as in the 19th Century.[6]

They would have seen it coming had they studied history, or even better Scripture, which warns nations and individuals of the consequences of abandoning God.

One can read the English translation of Solzhenitsyn's entire address at *www.americanrhetoric.com/speeches/alexander solzhenitsynharvard.htm*, and it's worth taking the time to read it all. Don't just read these speeches and weep. Read them and repent for yourself and on behalf of our nation.

NOTES

Introduction

1. John Glubb, *The Fate of Empires and Search for Survival* (Edinburgh: William Blackwood & Sons, 1976, 1977), *http://people.uncw.edu /kozloffm/glubb.pdf*.
2. Cal Thomas, *What Works: Common Sense Solutions for a Stronger America* (Grand Rapids: Zondervan, 2014).
3. Glubb, *The Fate of Empires,* 24.
4. Ibid.
5. Ibid.
6. Ibid.
7. Ibid.
8. In his address to Western ambassadors on November 8, 1956, in the Polish embassy in Moscow.
9. Joe Carter, "Canadian Supreme Court Ruling Has Implications for Christian Witness," *Gospel Coalition* (March 6, 2013), *www .thegospelcoalition.org/article/canadian-supreme-court-ruling-has -implications-for-christian-witness/*.

Chapter 1: The Persian Empire: Today a Shell of Its Great Past

1. See 2 Chronicles 36:22–23 as well as Ezra 1.
2. "Greco-Persian Wars," *Encyclopaedia Britannica* (last updated March 18, 2019), *www.britannica.com/event/Greco-Persian-Wars*.
3. Peter Davidson, "Achaemenid Empire," *Ancient History Encyclopedia* (February 11, 2011), *www.ancient.eu/Achaemenid_Empire/*.
4. Ibid.
5. Mehrdad Kia, *The Persian Empire: A Historical Encyclopedia* (Santa Barbara: ABC-CLIO, 2016), 127.
6. Modern totalitarian societies, notably Communist ones, have done the

same, but their military mostly keep a lid on the people so any protest, not to mention a revolt, is quickly and brutally extinguished. Recall the Tiananmen Square student demonstration for freedom in June 1989, which was rapidly and violently put down by the Beijing government.

7. 1 Timothy 6:10.

8. Matthew 7:12.

9. Original copies were distributed in China, long before the days of digital publishing and Amazon.com. China Books and Periodicals released an edition available in the US market in 1990, called *Quotations from Chairman Mao Tse-Tung*.

10. Howard Butt, *The Velvet Covered Brick: Christian Leadership in an Age of Rebellion* (New York: Harper and Row, 1963).

Chapter 2: The Roman Empires: Yes, It Really Burned

1. A contemporary of Jesus of Nazareth, and his name is recorded in Scripture.

2. Joshua J. Mark, "Roman Empire," *Ancient History Encyclopedia* (March 22, 2018), *www.ancient.eu/Roman_Empire/*.

3. "Roman Republic," *Encyclopaedia Britannica* (last updated April 3, 2018), *www.britannica.com/place/Roman-Republic*.

4. Erin Wayman, "The Secrets of Ancient Rome's Buildings," *Smithsonian* (November 16, 2011), *www.smithsonianmag.com/history/the-secrets-of-ancient-romes-buildings-234992/*.

5. Mark Cartwright, "Trade in the Roman World," *Ancient History Encyclopedia* (April 12, 2018), *www.ancient.eu/article/638/trade-in-the-roman-world/*.

6. Adrienne Bernhard, "Ancient Rome's Sinful City at the Bottom of the Sea," *BBC* (January 5, 2018), *www.bbc.com/travel/story/20180104-ancient-romes-sinful-city-at-the-bottom-of-the-sea*.

7. Nick Squires, "What Led to the Fall of the Roman Empire?" *Telegraph* (April 8, 2011), *www.telegraph.co.uk/news/worldnews/europe/italy/8438599/What-led-to-the-fall-of-the-Roman-Empire.html*.

8. You can access Gibbon's work for free online in various places, including *www.historyguide.org/intellect/gibbon_decline.html*.

Chapter 3: The Byzantine Empire: Officially Christian

1. Timothy E. Gregory, *A History of Byzantium*, 2nd ed. (Blackwell, 2010), 57–59.

2. "5 Major Accomplishments of Justinian," *HRF* (n.d.), *https://health research funding.org/5-major-accomplishments-of-justinian/*.

3. Ibid.

4. Ibid.

5. Barbara J. Ilie, "Libraries and Book Culture of the Byzantine Empire," *Medievalists.net* (n.d.), *www.medievalists.net/2012/04/libraries-and -book-culture-of-the-byzantine-empire/*.

6. "How Hagia Sophia Was Built," *Medievalists.net* (n.d.), *www.medievalists .net/2015/08/how-hagia-sophia-was-built/*.

7. John Bagnel Bury, *A History of the Later Roman Empire from Arcadius to Irene* (Adamant Media Corporation, 2005), 251.

Chapter 4: The Arab Empire: Muhammad's Followers

1. Michael Ray, "Battle of Tours," *Encyclopaedia Britannica* (last updated June 13, 2019), *www.britannica.com/event/Battle-of-Tours -732*.

2. Elizabeth Williams, "Trade and Commercial Activity in the Byzantine and Early Islamic Middle East," *The Met* (May 2012), *www.metmuseum.org/toah/hd/coin/hd_coin.htm*.

3. Mohamed Elmasry, "Ink of a Scholar Is More Holier Than the Blood of a Martyr," *IslamiCity* (October 29, 2015), *www.islamicity.org/3137 /ink-of-a-scholar-is-more-holier-than-the-blood-of-a-martyr/*.

4. Ian Frazier, "Invaders," *New Yorker* (April 25, 2005), *www.newyorker .com/magazine/2005/04/25/invaders-3*.

5. Dennis Overbye, "How Islam Won and Lost the Lead in Science," *New York Times* (October 30, 2001), *www.nytimes.com/2001/10/30 /science/how-islam-won-and-lost-the-lead-in-science.html*.

6. Hillel Ofek, "Why the Arabic World Turned Away from Science," *New Atlantis* (Winter 2011), *www.thenewatlantis.com/publications /why-the-arabic-world-turned-away-from-science*.

Chapter 5: The Spanish Empire: How the Mighty Doth Fall

1. "Ferdinand Magellan," *Mariners' Museum and Park* (n.d.), *http:// exploration.marinersmuseum.org/subject/ferdinand-magellan/*.

2. Haley Crum, "The Man Who Sailed the World," *Smithsonian.com* (May 31, 2007), *www.smithsonianmag.com/history/the-man-who -sailed-the-world-155994800/*.

3. "Ferdinand Magellan," *Mariners' Museum and Park*.

4. R. R. Palmer, Joel Colton, and Lloyd S. Kramer, *A History of the Modern World*, 9th ed. (Boston: McGraw-Hill, 2002).

5. "Philip II," *Encyclopaedia Britannica* (last updated July 21, 2019), *www.britannica.com/place/Spain/Philip-II#ref70403*.

6. "Spain in 1600," *Encyclopaedia Britannica* (last updated July 21, 2019), *www.britannica.com/place/Spain/Spain-in-1600#ref70407*.

7. "Senator Everett McKinley Dirksen Dies," *United States Senate* (September 7, 1969), *www.senate.gov/artandhistory/history/minute /Senator_Everett_Mckinley_Dirksen_Dies.htm*.

8. "Culture," *Dictionary.com* (n.d.), *www.dictionary.com/browse/culture*.

9. Ibid.

10. "Philip IV's Reign," *Encyclopaedia Britannica* (last updated July 21, 2019), *www.britannica.com/place/Spain/Philip-IVs-reign*.

11. Bernard Moses, "The Economic Condition of Spain in the Sixteenth Century," *Journal of Political Economy* 1, no. 4 (September 1893): 531–34.

Chapter 6: The Ottoman Empire: Winners and Losers

1. Suzan Yalman, "The Age of Süleyman 'the Magnificent' (r. 1520–1566)" (based on original work by Linda Komaroff), *The Met* (October 2002), *www.metmuseum.org/toah/hd/suly/hd_suly.htm*.

2. "Magnificent No More," *Economist* (January 27, 2011), *www.economist .com/node/18013830*.

3. "Suleiman the Magnificent's Tomb Believed to Have Been Found in Hungary," *Guardian* (December 9, 2015), *www.theguardian.com /science/2015/dec/09/suleiman-the-magnificent-tomb-hungary*.

4. "Cultural Life," *Encyclopaedia Britannica* (last updated July 19, 2019), *www.britannica.com/place/Macedonia/Cultural-life#ref42800*.

5. Thomas Madden, "The Real History of the Crusades," *CatholiCity* (April 1, 2002), *www.catholicity.com/commentary/madden/03463.html*.

6. Stephen Starr, "Istanbul's Hagia Sophia Is at the Centre of a Battle for Turkey's Soul," *Irish Times* (January 2, 2018), *www.irishtimes.com /news/world/europe/istanbul-s-hagia-sophia-is-at-the-centre-of-a-battle -for-turkey-s-soul-1.3342259*.

7. Ibid.

8. "The Resurgence of Islam: The Response of the Church," *LightSource* (n.d.), *www.lightsource.com/ministry/running-to-win/articles/the -resurgence-of-islam-the-response-of-the-church--16530.html*.

9. Ibid.

10. Dimitrie Cantemir, *The History of the Growth and Decay of the Othman Empire* (London: J. J. and P. Knapton, 1734), 252.

Chapter 7: The British Empire: Where the Sun Never Sets

1. John Glubb, *The Fate of Empires and Search for Survival* (Edinburgh: William Blackwood & Sons, 1976, 1977), 6.

2. Ibid., 4.

3. Richard North Patterson, "The Vision of George H. W. Bush," *HuffPost* (December 29, 2015), *www.huffingtonpost.com/richard-north-patterson/the-vision-of-george-hw-b_b_8868536.html*.

4. Martin Kettle, "David Cameron Is Wise to Want to Be the New Stanley Baldwin," *Guardian* (February 12, 2014), *www.theguardian.com/commentisfree/2014/feb/12/david-cameron-new-stanley-baldwin-tory*.

5. Anne Perkins, "Theresa May's Paralysis on the Big Issues Has Echoes in History," *Guardian* (August 2, 2017), *www.theguardian.com/commentisfree/2017/aug/02/theresa-may-stanley-baldwin*.

6. Victor Davis Hanson, "Obama Is America's Version of Stanley Baldwin," *National Review* (April 13, 2017), *www.nationalreview.com/article/446688/obama-foreign-policy-trumps-situation-resemble-britain-wwii*.

7. Jude T. Wanniski, *Financial Analysts Journal* (January/February 1980): 20.

8. Ibid.

9. Approximately 1837–1901, the years of Queen Victoria's reign.

10. Donna Loftus, "The Rise of the Victorian Middle Class," *BBC* (last updated February 17, 2011), *www.bbc.co.uk/history/british/victorians/middle_classes_01.shtml*.

11. Martha Kirby, "Too Much of a Good Thing? Society, Affluence and Obesity in Britain, 1940–1970," *eSharp* (2012), *www.gla.ac.uk/media/media_228377_en.pdf*.

12. Dominic Sandbrook, "Is Europe Committing Suicide?" *Daily Mail* (May 20, 2017), *www.pressreader.com/uk/daily-mail/20170520/283347587124920*.

13. Ibid.

14. Ibid.

15. Guy Adams, "Inside Britain's Sharia Courts," *Daily Mail* (December 13, 2015), *www.dailymail.co.uk/news/article-3358625/Inside-Britain*

-s-Sharia-courts-EIGHTY-FIVE-Islamic-courts-dispensing-justice
-UK-special-investigation-really-goes-doors-shock-core.html.

16. Ibid.

17. The full text is available for free online in numerous places, including
*www.telegraph.co.uk/comment/3643826/Enoch-Powells-Rivers-of
-Blood-speech.html*.

18. Consider Deuteronomy 10:19, as well as Leviticus 19:34, Matthew
25:35, and Hebrews 13:2.

Chapter 8: The Russian Empire: From Orthodoxy to Communism

1. John L. H. Keep, "Nicholas II: Tsar of Russia," *Encyclopaedia Britannica*
(last updated July 13, 2019), *www.britannica.com/biography/Nicholas-II
-tsar-of-Russia*.

2. Chris Banescu, "Men Have Forgotten God: Alexander Soltzhenitsyn,"
Orthodox Christianity (July 18, 2011), *http://orthochristian.com/47643
.html*.

3. Ibid., emphasis in original.

4. "Catherine II," *Biography* (last updated June 21, 2019), *www.biography
.com/people/catherine-ii-9241622*.

5. Ibid.

Chapter 9: The United States: 1776–?

1. Richard Heilman, "A Plea for Intolerance by Venerable Fulton J. Sheen,"
Roman Catholic Man (April 9, 2016), *www.romancatholicman.com/a
-plea-for-intolerance-by-venerable-fulton-j-sheen/*.

2. "Document: Speech on the 150th Anniversary of the Declaration
of Independence," *Teaching American History* (n.d.), *http://teaching
americanhistory.org/library/document/speech-on-the-occasion-of-the-one
-hundred-and-fiftieth-anniversary-of-the-declaration-of-independence/*.

3. Charles Stanley, "A Passion to Serve Him," *InTouch Ministries* (n.d.),
www.intouch.org/listen/featured/a-passion-to-serve-him-part-1 and
www.intouch.org/listen/featured/a-passion-to-serve-him-part-2.

4. Patrick J. Buchanan, "America's 2nd Civil War," *WND* (August 17,
2017), *www.wnd.com/2017/08/americas-2nd-civil-war-2/*.

5. Carl Henry, "The Crisis of Modern Learning," *Imprimis* 13, no. 2 (February 1984), *https://imprimis.hillsdale.edu/the-crisis-of-modern-learning/*.

6. Ibid.

7. Scotty Smith, "Quotes from C. S. Lewis' Screwtape Letters," *Gospel Coalition* (July 13, 2008), *www.thegospelcoalition.org/blogs/scotty -smith/quotes-from-c-s-lewis-screwtape-letters/.*

8. Robert J. Samuelson, "Trump Is Not Destiny. Here's What Is," *Washington Post* (June 11, 2017), *www.washingtonpost.com/opinions /trump-is-not-destiny-heres-what-is/2017/06/11/1dc9f7c6-4d33-11e7 -9669-250d0b15f83b_story.html?utm_term=.928ebb06424b.*

9. Ibid.

10. Carlos Lozada, "Will the West Survive Trump?" *Washington Post* (June 15, 2017), *www.washingtonpost.com/news/book-party/wp/2017 /06/15/will-the-west-survive-trump/?utm_term=.86730f54cc76.*

11. Jose A. DelReal and Scott Clement, "Rural Divide," *Washington Post* (June 17, 2017), *www.washingtonpost.com/graphics/2017/national /rural-america/?utm_term=.1304e4895295.*

12. Ibid.

13. Rod Dreher, *The Benedict Option* (New York: Penguin Random House, 2017).

14. Rod Dreher, "Critics of the Benedict Option," *American Conservative* (July 8, 2015), *www.theamericanconservative.com/dreher/critics-of-the -benedict-option/.*

15. Rod Dreher, "Trump Can't Save American Christianity," *New York Times* (August 2, 2017), *www.nytimes.com/2017/08/02/opinion /trump-scaramucci-evangelical-christian.html.*

16. R. Albert Mohler Jr., "Moralistic Therapeutic Deism—The New American Religion," *Christian Post* (April 18, 2005), *www.christian post.com/news/moralistic-therapeutic-deism-the-new-american-religion -6266/.*

17. Ibid.

18. Dreher, "Trump Can't Save American Christianity."

19. Alex Witchel, "Father Rabbit," *New York Times* (November 22, 1992), *www.nytimes.com/1992/11/22/style/father-rabbit.html.*

20. "Direction of Country," *Real Clear Politics* (n.d.), *www.realclearpolitics .com/epolls/other/direction_of_country-902.html.*

Appendix 1: Bonus Cameos

1. Alina Polyakova, "Europe's Failing Dream," *American Interest* (September 14, 2015), *www.the-american-interest.com/2015/09/14 /europes-failing-dream/.*

2. "Has the German State Lost Control?" *Spiegel Online* (January 21, 2016), *www.spiegel.de/international/germany/germans-ask-if-country-is-still-safe-after-cologne-attacks-a-1073165.html*.

Appendix 2: A Prophet Ignored

1. Aleksandr Solzhenitsyn, "Godlessness: The First Step to the Gulag," Templeton Prize Lecture, London (May 10, 1983), emphasis mine. This text appears by permission of the Aleksandr Soltzhenitsyn Estate. All rights reserved.

Appendix 3: The Prophet's Second Warning

1. Alexandr Solzhenitsyn, "A World Split Apart," Harvard University commencement address, delivered June 8, 1978, *American Rhetoric* (n.d.), *www.americanrhetoric.com/speeches/alexandersolzhenitsyn harvard.htm*.

2. Ibid.

3. Ibid.

4. Ibid.

5. Ibid.

6. Ibid.